POETRY COMPETITION
FOR 11-18 YEAR-OLDS

POP!
The Power Of Poetry

# Southern England

Edited by Steve Twelvetree

 Young**Writers**

First published in Great Britain in 2006 by:
Young Writers
Remus House
Coltsfoot Drive
Peterborough
PE2 9JX
Telephone: 01733 890066
Website: www.youngwriters.co.uk

SB ISBN 1 84602 388 2

# Foreword

This year, the Young Writers' *POP! - The Power Of Poetry* competition proudly presents a showcase of the best poetic talent selected from thousands of up-and-coming writers nationwide.

Young Writers was established in 1991 to promote the reading and writing of poetry within schools and to the young of today. Our books nurture and inspire confidence in the ability of young writers and provide a snapshot of poems written in schools and at home by budding poets of the future.

The thought, effort, imagination and hard work put into each poem impressed us all and the task of selecting poems was a difficult but nevertheless enjoyable experience.

We hope you are as pleased as we are with the final selection and that you and your family continue to be entertained with *POP! Southern England* for many years to come.

# Contents

Ciara McNamee  (11)                           23
Christopher Nicholas  (12)                    24
Lucinda Needham  (11)                         25
Loretta Harcombe  (11)                        26
Cora Morrissey  (12)                          27
Lauren Nicoll  (11)                           28
Victoria Dale  (11)                           29
Paige Nolan  (12)                             30
Courtney Bailey  (11)                         31
Georgina-Emily Cook  (11)                     32
Madison Taylor  (11)                          33
Lucy Howell  (12)                             34

## Bedgebury School, Goudhurst

Hermione Cameron  (12)                        35
Katie Wooding Jones  (12)                     35
Eva Tang  (12)                                36
Abi Firth  (12)                               37
Kayleigh Gowen-Smith  (14)                    38

## Hartsdown Technology College, Margate

Calum Georgiou  (12)                          38
Aysha Begum  (13)                             39
Laura Hodges  (12)                            39
Hannah Kerrigan  (14)                         40
Fraser Lawrance  (13)                         40
Matthew Brown  (15)                           41
Tony Handley  (12)                            41
Luke Alexander  (14)                          42
Robert Payn  (13)                             42
Amelia Acaster  (12)                          43
Matt Leighton  (15)                           43
Katherine Lowe  (11)                          44
Rebecca Rhodes  (13)                          44
Kyle Gleeson  (13)                            45
Remy Glendinning  (13)                        45
Matthew Reed  (12)                            46
Miranda Spencer  (14)                         46
Amy McGregor  (13)                            47
Laura Cheshire  (13)                          47
Daniel Pellegrini  (12)                       48

Chloe McAteer  (12)                              48
Eloise McGinley  (12)                            48
Natalie Culver  (12)                             49
James Bartlett-Smith  (12)                       49
Daniel Utteridge  (13)                           49
Rebecca Bedford  (12)                            50
Brandon Palmer  (12)                             50
Lauren Chapman  (13)                             50
Daniel Cass  (13)                                51
Lucy Gower  (12)                                 51

## Highcliffe School, Christchurch
Izzy Worrall  (11)                               52
Elaine Bell  (11)                                53
Chloe Bentall  (12)                              54
Hannah Elkins  (11)                              54
Robin Joynson  (11)                              55
Madeleine Daley-Brown  (11)                      55
Rachel Baker  (11)                               56

## Portchester School, Bournemouth
Jack Downs  (12)                                 56
Rowan Lee  (12)                                  57
Jamie Kascioglu  (12)                            58
Bradley Wilson  (12)                             59
Connor Daly  (12)                                60
Zachary Bradley  (12)                            61
James Keith  (15)                                61
Michael Sauget  (15)                             62
Henry Ho-Yin Cheung  (12)                        62
Kelsey Bennett  (12)                             63
Callum Ford  (15)                                63
Muhammad Waqas Ahmad  (12)                       64
Troy Stensel  (12)                               65
Felix Apalisok  (13)                             66
Charlie Cook  (12)                               66
Jon Packer  (12)                                 67
Jason Everitt  (12)                              67
Danny Supple  (13)                               68
Ben King  (12)                                   68
Michael Robertson  (12)                          69

| | |
|---|---|
| Sergio La Mantia  (12) | 69 |
| Sam Dargan  (13) | 70 |
| Shahibur Rahman  (12) | 71 |
| Joe Connor  (13) | 72 |
| William McDowell  (12) | 72 |
| Thomas Caullay  (12) | 73 |
| Kieran Lockyer  (12) | 73 |
| Logan Partridge  (16) | 74 |
| Josh Kaye  (15) | 75 |
| Connor Clark  (12) | 75 |
| Luke Bayliss  (15) | 76 |
| Joe Jones  (15) | 76 |
| Leo Abate  (15) | 77 |
| Michael Nicholls  (15) | 77 |
| David Henon  (15) | 78 |
| Luke Tanswell  (15) | 79 |
| Donald Dowling  (15) | 79 |
| Lloyd Harkcom  (15) | 80 |
| James Ferrett  (15) | 80 |
| Daniel Payne  (15) | 81 |
| Ben Heathman  (15) | 81 |
| Kiran Patel  (15) | 82 |
| Samuel Cooke  (16) | 82 |
| Nick Woolner  (15) | 83 |
| David Love  (15) | 83 |
| Billy Player  (13) | 84 |
| James Plunkett  (11) | 84 |
| David Pettet  (11) | 85 |
| James Cooper  (11) | 85 |
| Kit Moulding  (15) | 86 |
| George Lawrence  (15) | 86 |
| Matthew Watkins  (11) | 87 |
| Matthew Sacchi  (11) | 87 |
| Matthew Allen  (15) | 88 |
| Ewan Leckie  (15) | 88 |
| James Lofts  (16) | 89 |
| Christian Ridout  (12) | 89 |
| Ashley Calderwood  (12) | 90 |
| Sam Le Feaux  (12) | 91 |
| Haydon Palmer  (16) | 91 |
| Kristyen Denham  (16) | 92 |

## Regents Park Community College, Southampton

| | |
|---|---|
| Katie Beckingham (14) | 92 |
| Rachael Murray (13) | 93 |
| Jemma Gilbert (13) | 94 |
| Carmen Jones (13) | 94 |
| Jade Mintrim (13) | 95 |
| Laura Morrell (13) | 95 |
| Beth Cooke (13) | 96 |
| Katrina Loizou (13) | 97 |
| Eloise Lavington (13) | 98 |
| Ella Dixon (13) | 98 |
| Libby Thornton (13) | 99 |
| Maryam Anibaba (13) | 99 |

## Ryeish Green School, Reading

| | |
|---|---|
| Danielle Meakin (15) | 100 |
| Hannah Crozier (15) | 100 |
| Natasha Turner (14) | 101 |
| Victoria Aldridge (15) | 101 |
| Laura Russell (15) | 102 |
| Juhi Saini (15) | 102 |

## St Antony's Leweston School, Sherborne

| | |
|---|---|
| Daisy Skepelhorn (12) | 103 |
| Charlotte Walters (11) | 103 |
| Hattie Field (11) | 104 |
| Hennie Helliwell (11) | 105 |
| Taliska Baden (11) | 106 |
| Chloë Henderson (13) | 106 |
| Jade Letts | 107 |
| Monica Sanchez (13) | 107 |
| Florence Pisani (11) | 108 |
| Isabelle Barber (12) | 109 |
| Rowan Skellern (11) | 109 |
| Chloé Taylor (11) | 110 |
| Daisy Crichton (12) | 110 |
| Rachel Hill (11) | 111 |
| Hanayo Uchida (14) | 111 |
| Violet Thompson (13) | 112 |
| Kitty Whittell (11) | 113 |

**St Gabriel's School, Newbury**

Georgia Hawkesworth  (12)                               160
Lucy Meredith  (11)                                     160
Rhianna MacGregor  (12)                                 161
Ellie Baxter  (11)                                      161

## Sherborne School for Girls, Sherborne
Francesca Tennant  (13)                                 162
Rachael Ellis  (13)                                     162
Emily Rainbow  (13)                                     163
Georgina Bolton Carter  (13)                            163
Pippa Jenkins  (13)                                     164
Chloë E Scott  (13)                                     164
Georgia Horrocks  (14)                                  165
Alice Hayes  (13)                                       165
Natasha Marks  (13)                                     166
Alice Maltby  (13)                                      166
Antonia Hollis  (13)                                    167
Louise Crowley  (13)                                    167
Tessa Astbury  (14)                                     168
Elizabeth Norman  (13)                                  168

## Sir Joseph Williamson Mathematical School, Rochester
Thomas Starling  (12)                                   169
Ben Shrubsole  (15)                                     170
James Tutt  (13)                                        170
Tommy Nundy  (13)                                       171
Ben Stroud  (12)                                        171
Matthew Roberts  (12)                                   172
Alex Brown  (11)                                        173
Sam Brown  (11)                                         174
Sam Pepper  (11)                                        175
Jack Poynter  (12)                                      175
Jonathan Nunn  (12)                                     176
Samuel Seed  (11)                                       176
Jamie Cogle  (11)                                       177
Kyle Hellemans  (12)                                    178
Matthew Maybury  (11)                                   179
Andrew Fenton  (11)                                     180
Andrew Bowdery  (13)                                    180
Krishna Joshi  (11)                                     181
Ben Wellard  (11)                                       181

| | |
|---|---|
| Daniel Barker  (11) | 182 |
| Callum Burgess  (12) | 182 |
| James Spencer  (13) | 183 |
| Victor Williams  (14) | 183 |
| Joel Calder  (13) | 184 |
| Edward Brookes  (13) | 185 |
| Adam Owen  (14) | 186 |
| Casey Legg  (13) | 186 |
| Thomas Selves  (12) | 187 |
| Tola Adesina  (17) | 187 |
| Graeme Struthers  (14) | 188 |
| Ryan Evans  (13) | 188 |
| Matthew Wren  (11) | 189 |
| Jonathan Beck  (12) | 189 |
| Tom Heath  (12) | 190 |
| Harry Stevens  (13) | 191 |
| Ben Elder  (13) | 192 |
| Joe Evans  (14) | 193 |
| Harshal Patel  (11) | 193 |
| Tom Smith  (13) | 194 |
| Conor Laker  (11) | 194 |
| Thomas Mo  (13) | 195 |
| Remy Holmes  (13) | 195 |
| Paul Wilson  (15) | 196 |
| Samuel Shackleton  (11) | 197 |
| Alex Daykin  (11) | 198 |
| Lewis Moran  (13) | 199 |
| Harrison Land  (11) | 199 |
| Connor Ashenden  (13) | 200 |
| Thomas Lloyd  (11) | 200 |
| Kierran Boden  (12) | 201 |
| Julian McManus  (12) | 201 |
| Tom Seed  (13) | 202 |
| Zeshan Mirza  (11) | 202 |
| Talos Tsavellas  (13) | 203 |
| Phillip Vidler  (12) | 203 |
| Lewis Bailey  (11) | 204 |
| Aaron Dimmick  (14) | 204 |
| Ryan Dennis  (11) | 205 |
| Alex Mortley  (12) | 205 |
| Liam Dooley  (11) | 206 |
| Sam Heyes  (11) | 207 |

# The Poems

# The Ghost

The transparent person, who said he was a host,
Was actually found out to be a ghost,
He knocked on our door, with an invitation,
It really was full of Hallowe'en creation.
I thought it was great, I wanted to go,
It was sure to be a fantastic show,
So I got in the car and drove to the house,
The place was just as quiet as a mouse.
I went to the door and I was terrified,
The hairy old knocker nearly made me cry,
The door opened, all by itself,
All that was in front of me was a shelf.
I saw an old key and picked it up,
And then all of a sudden the door was shut,
I got twisted round and taken into a room,
And then all of a sudden I heard a *BOOM!*
A mythical ghost, an ugly thing,
It took hold of me and I dropped like a pin,
I thought I was dead,
By the way, he had chopped of my head,
There was no blood it was nice and easy,
But I did feel a little bit queasy,
My head rolled to the left, it rolled to the right,
I thought it was going to roll all night!
I slowly walked over, my head was on the floor,
I picked it up and walked out the door,
'That's the last time I'm coming to your house,' I screamed,
Well, we'll have to wait until next Hallowe'en!

**Alice Gillespie  (11)**
**Avonbourne School, Bournemouth**

# Something Is Out!

It's out tonight
The moon's in sight

There is its howling
It is still prowling

Keep your windows shut
It's eaten next-door's mutt

Don't try to trap it
It's killed Mrs Tall's rabbit

Blood drips from its teeth
Do not think it's a thief

Be warned it's out tonight
The werewolf is in sight.

**Annabel Wilson  (12)**
**Avonbourne School, Bournemouth**


# Up On The Moon

Up on the moon how I wish I could fly,
Cos high up in the sky,
There sitting on the moon,
Is a complete and utter loon!
He does a little dance like he's in a trance,
How I wish I could fly,
Cos high up in the sky,
There sitting on the moon,
Is a complete and utter loon!
He sings a *daba daba doo a looba looba loo!*
He runs around laughing, I sure think he's crazy!
But one thing I know for sure, he's definitely not lazy!
How I wish I could fly,
Cos there's a man high up in the dark blue sky!

**Abbie Robinson  (12)**
**Bay House School, Gosport**

# My Human-Like Pizza

I bought her from Asda,
She looked quite divine,
But now she lays dead,
In that stomach of mine.

I loved her pink hair,
And her black olive eyes,
But now she lays dead,
In that stomach of mine.

Her cheese-like skin,
And her sweet, corn-like fringe,
But now she lays dead,
In that stomach of mine.

Her goofy-like teeth,
Her red cheeks like tomato,
But now she lays dead,
In that stomach of mine.

I only had one pizza left,
I used to have nine,
But now they lay dead,
In that stomach of mine.

I always name my pizzas,
My last one was called Kelly,
But now she lays dead,
In my huge, greedy belly.

**Holly Pattison  (11)**
**Bay House School, Gosport**

# A Day In The Life Of A Lion And A Snow Cub

As the snow cubs play in the snow,
The shimmering sun begins to glow,
So Mum goes out and gets a treat,
For the snow cubs, is it sweet?
She finds some fish on the shore,
And her eyes begin to pour,
For she has lost a loved one,
And he got chased by a poacher with a gun,
She gives the lonesome cubs their tea,
And wonders where her cub could be.

As the fuzzy lion wakes,
Some juicy meat to his wife he takes,
He gets the cubs up and washed,
And in the water the cubs slosh,
But when the cubs are shaking dry,
He sees a hyena from his eye,
The hyena whacks the lion's mane,
So the cub hits back, pathetic and lame,
The lion roars and hits him back,
And the hyena falls down with a crack.

**Caroline King  (11)**
**Bay House School, Gosport**


# Face

Peekers, peekers, blink and glare,
Peekers, peekers, wink and stare.
Nozzle, nozzle, sniff the smell,
This incredible nozzle smells so well.
Twitchers, twitchers listen near,
As a soft warm sound creeps down your ear,
Gossip box, gossip box stays open, never locks!

**Naomi Harper  (12)**
**Bay House School, Gosport**

# A Trip Inside My Brain

Take a trip inside my brain,
But I warn you it could get very insane!
Your first stop is the imaginary zoo,
Where foxes in dungarees sleep in goo!

Next take a wood and combine it with a bog,
It equals a very fierce, flying kung fu log!
Now there's a sound I can always name,
It's a nanny pig on a Zimmer frame!

Now for this bit keep your limbs inside my brain,
Unless you wish to be in great pain!
Because we're passing Mr Nidum with his 12 foot nosey,
But just imagine the size of his 10 foot bogies!

The last place to go is not a bore,
Because you can eat deformed cabbages all the more!
And if you didn't like it I'll get my own back,
Because you're in my world and I don't have to send you back!

So, now you're out I ask 'Did you enjoy it?'
And why are you having an epileptic fit?
But isn't it weird that whomever sees my brain,
Eventually ends up going insane!

**Jack Elshaw  (12)**
**Bay House School, Gosport**


# The Bully

Bully doesn't like me,
But he likes to kick and punch me.
The bully doesn't like me,
I hope he goes away.

He may call me Bugs Bunny,
I know he thinks it's funny.
It always goes too far,
I wish there was a getaway car.

**Lindsey Jackson  (11)**
**Bay House School, Gosport**

# Rainbow Wiggler!

Rainbow wiggler moves slowly and steadily,
He creeps past danger very cleverly,
He waits and waits for many days,
Blinded by the bright sunrays.

Every day and every night,
'Danger! Danger! The birds have  taken flight,'
Everyone beware tonight,
Tonight I think we're in for a fright.

Watching the birds fly in the sky,
Every day of the year they just ask why,
A caterpillar has died and we don't know who,
Whoever killed him, we need Scooby-Doo.

That's the end of my poem now bye,
That dull old caterpillar is now a butterfly,
My poem's about a caterpillar's lifetime,
And if you have noticed it even rhymes.

**Robbie Hale  (11)**
**Bay House School, Gosport**


# My Best Mate And Me

Love the colour purple,
Both have blue eyes,
We both hate mushroom pies.

Football rocks,
We both play musical instruments,
Love stripy socks,
Both hate camping in tents.

We both like pasta in sauce,
Love Diet Coke,
Of course,
And play practical jokes.

**Lucy Langston  (11)**
**Bay House School, Gosport**

# The Jibberabbersmabbaladdabangboo Land

*(Inspired by 'Jabberwocky' by Lewis Carroll)*

The Jibberabberang has teeth that go clang,
The Smiggasmaggasmoo has feet that go *Whoo!*
The Liggalaggalongs have hair that really pongs,
In Jibberabbersmabbaladdabangboo Land.

The Smallagallamaldives have nails like sharp knives
The Doobagoobaloobalat is the size of a gnat,
The Shallalalalaladongs have mouths like tongs
In Jibberabbersmabbaladdabangboo Land.

The Jammalamagammadam has legs made out of ham,
With the Slimbagimbadimbachis a wash wouldn't go a miss,
The Slimmadimagimmachip has a very, very large lip
In Jibberabbersmabbaladdabangboo Land.

**Jack Hiron  (11)**
**Bay House School, Gosport**


# Flowers

Some flowers are skinny, some flowers are tall,
Some flowers are fat and others are small.
The colours are great, the colours are wild,
They stand out well, like a screaming child.
Red is for roughness, but cerise is for sorrow,
Some are white, like my fluffy pillow.
Blue is for blindness, perfection means pink,
Some colours are weird, some make you think.
Orange is outstanding, purple means at play,
Black is for boldness and bravery all day.
Brown is bewitched, and yellow is for yearning,
Green stands for greatness, which is everlasting.
So that is my poem all about flowers,
And some of them even have mystical powers.

**Amber Christie Blair  (11)**
**Bay House School, Gosport**

# Time Of The Year

B irthdays are fun
I like birthdays
R unning to the bowling aisle
T hen we play!
H it the pins
D own they go
A nd it's a strike!
Y es! What a shot!

E aster is the time of the year we get Easter eggs
A n Easter egg is made of chocolate
S mashing the eggs must be fun
T hen we eat them one by one!
E aster is fun
R un around then eat!

C hristmas is fun
H aving presents
R unning downstairs to peek
I like Christmas
S itting with a present
T aking pictures
M aking cards
A t Christmas
S ometimes we get what we want!

**Jordan Bayles  (11)**
**Bay House School, Gosport**

# Louder Than . . .

Louder than elephants stomping,
Louder than giants chomping.

Louder than planes crashing,
Louder than windows smashing.

Louder than hooligans screaming,
And even louder than Wembley screaming,
This is my brother plus more.

**Ryan Hammond  (11)**
**Bay House School, Gosport**

# The Life Of Spiders On The Planet Kearth

Spiders small and spiders *BIG,*
Grandma spiders wearing wigs.
Spiders start out very small,
And stay with their mothers until they crawl.

Some have oddly coloured spots,
Which they show-off a lot.
The spider,
Is a hider.

While the spider's mouth,
Is always out.
Some swish on their webs,
And others go *whump* on their heads.

There are spiders that kill,
And cowards that run to the hills.
People are scared when they should be not,
Only 20 types kill, but they kill a lot.

So you now must not be scared,
Because they live up in space somewhere.
You're lucky down here on planet Earth,
You won't want to be near a spider on planet *Kearth!*

**Callum Stewart  (12)**
**Bay House School, Gosport**


# Something Sweet Like Love

Something sweet like love,
All we need is a shove,
We don't need another,
Because we have each other,
It's like we were sent from above.

**Lauren Miskelly  (11)**
**Bay House School, Gosport**

# Horses

*(This poem was written to support the RSPCA)*

Some horses work hard,
Pulling a cart,
And at the end of the day,
They go home.

Not all horses live like that.

Some stay alone in a field,
Munching on grass,
Others stay stabled,
With no food or drink,
In other places,
There are some that are hurt,
For they have been beaten and bruised,
Then left,
Dying,
Alone and cold.

How do you hurt these beautiful beasts?

But out there people do,
They turn from pretty, sweet and loving animals,
Into mad and frightened things,
Whose eyes are filled with fear,
And then someone comes,
To give them to people who will love and care for them,
And they turn back to enjoyable beasts,
Thanks to the love that they have received,
But not all are so lucky,
Out there,
It's still going on.

**Danielle Ray  (12)**
**Bay House School, Gosport**

# Flamengo

Flamengo is coming to get me,
I come upon its habitat home and it goes
*'Goar roar I'm going to kill you*
*You mark my words!'*

Oh no oh my the dangerous beastly
Flamengo is after me!
What shall I do? What shall I do?
Should I go and live in another country?
Should I go back to my house and never come out?
*No I will kill the vicious beast!*

I shall hunt the beast down,
I shall go in the gruesome Forbidden Forest!
I will get the most vicious sword there is!
I will chop its gruesome head off and chop it up!

I walk into the forest,
He immediately smells me coming,
He says, 'It is time for me to kill you.'
'Right back at ya Evil,' I said,
'Let's get this party started right now.'

He grabs me and puts me high in the sky,
I grab my sword and stab him in the neck,
He squeals and roars and falls on to the floor,
I stab him through the heart,
Blood comes flying out everywhere,
I have finally killed the Flamengo beast.

**Zoe Lewis  (11)**
**Bay House School, Gosport**

# Knickers

Knickers
Old-fashioned long johns,
Big bloomers and briefs,
Polka-dot pants,
Small and stretchy can be a grief!
Huge hot pants,
And lacy linens,
Baggy boxers hang down to your knee knockers!
Mine are droopy draws!
What are yours?
Some keep you warm in the winter,
Some keep you cool in the summer,
Types of knickers,
Just get,
Funnier
And
*Funnier!*

**Amy Tungatt  (11)**
**Bay House School, Gosport**


# Bugatti Veyron

The Bugatti Veyron,
It's beautiful.
1001 bhp packed on,
And it defies friction's pull.

Fast as hell,
Fancy leather,
It also has a CD player.

One fine day I'll buy it,
In a brilliant colour.
Although I highly doubt it,
It costs a million dollars

**Hugh Heyworth  (11)**
**Bay House School, Gosport**

# My Dog Tilly

Ears as big as elephants' ears,
Eyes as shiny as stars,
Fluffy like a teddy bear,
Teeth as sharp as daggers,
Cuddly as a kitten,
Sneaky as a leopard stalking his prey,
Nose as black as a storm cloud,
Tongue as slimy as a slug,
Paws as big as tigers' claws,
Tail fluffy like a feather duster,
Fast as a cheetah,
Bark as loud as a car horn,
Shaped like a lion cub,
Smells nice and sweet,
Brown and white like a cow,
Whiskers like a soft brush.

**Emily Smith  (11)**
**Bay House School, Gosport**


# My Dog

Tilly is my dog's name,
And catch is her game.
She is soft and fluffy,
And very friendly,
And I thought of her name!

She is kind to me,
And is always happy to see me,
She is nice and cuddly,
And she is playful as can be.

**Lucas Arnold  (11)**
**Bay House School, Gosport**

# Harry And Garry The Giant Tortoises

There is a giant tortoise called Harry,
Who has a friend called Garry,
They went to get ice cream,
And to watch a football team,
The team said, 'Go away,'
Harry and Garry asked why they couldn't stay,
'Because you're too big,' the team said,
So Harry and Garry went home,
But on the way Harry knocked over a gnome,
Harry got shouted at, he was sad,
Garry bumped into someone, the person was mad,
So Harry and Garry moved to the wild,
The weather there was mild,
Harry and Garry made a new friend,
Harry and Garry were on the mend,
Everyone liked them in the wild,
So Harry and Garry said, 'Can we stay?'
The animals said, 'Yes you may.'

**Sean Dibley (11)**
**Bay House School, Gosport**

# Hallowe'en

Children knocking on the door,
I see broomsticks on the floor,
People asking for some sweets,
Some are saying, 'Trick or treat?'

Some are asking for some more,
They act as if they're poor,
Some dress as witches,
Or Frankenstein with masks that have stitches.

Some neighbours get annoyed,
Every child should have enjoyed,
They should be keen,
*This is Hallowe'en!*

**Hilary Ho (11)**
**Bay House School, Gosport**

# Tigger Is A Tiger

Tigger is a bouncy tiger,
Who boings and jumps for glee.
He makes you smile all the while,
As he has a cool personality.

Tigger is an orange and black tiger,
Who has a lot of friends.
Who also likes honey, which makes him funny,
Till the honey pot ends!

Tigger is a generous tiger,
Who always has the time.
He is always happy to see people,
To make sure they are fine.

Tigger is a friendly tiger,
With Pooh, Piglet and Eeyore by his side.
He's cool eating honey with his crew,
The friends he can always find.

**Hayley Rutherford  (12)**
**Bay House School, Gosport**


# I Wish . . .

I wish I was a bird,
So I could soar over the land.

I wish I was a blue whale,
The biggest in the world.

I wish I was a cheetah,
The fastest in the land.

I wish I was the prime minister,
To make all the right choices.

I wish I was a great oak,
Hundreds of years old.

But I am glad I am myself,
Because I like myself a lot.

**Dan Irving  (11)**
**Bay House School, Gosport**

# Who Am I?

I floated up to the old wooden door,
Leaving nothing, not even a footprint on the muddy floor.

The wind was screaming, stabbing through me,
Like a gunshot, powerful, too fast to see.

The moonlight was beaming onto my blanket-like back,
Wrapping round me like a shiny bright sack.

The smell was damp, murky and bitter,
So bad, so foul, like mouldy litter.

Shadows swayed spookily from side to side,
Like ghosts on the prowl off they glide.

The forest was cold as I snuck on through,
With my shoulders hunched as I flew.

Creeping, seeking, but what for?
I'm on the move again one night, once more.

I am the mist, I prowl the land,
Covering the Earth with my clouded hand.

**Anna Hammond  (11)**
**Bay House School, Gosport**


# Winter

Snow coming down and
Laying a thick layer on the ground
Wearing thick coats and woolly hats
Making snow angels in the snow
Also, snowy snowmen silently sleeping
Whilst you wait for Christmas Day
The opening of presents in the morning
The roast turkey for tea
Remember winter only comes once a year
So, make the most of it just for you and me.

**Jazmin Huntington  (11)**
**Bay House School, Gosport**

# Cats Kennings

My cats are:
Dinner nickin'
Water splashin'
Mess makin'
Tail chasin'
Bigger growin'
Head bangin'
Active runnin'
Cute cuddlin'
Food eatin'
Great jumpin'
Always sleepin'

Sweet and lovable cats.

**Claire Wake (11)**
**Bay House School, Gosport**


# Wolves

Wolves,
I hear on a full moon,
Wolves,
I hear them howl,
Wolves,
Standing on the edge of the cliff,
Wolves,
They wait in the dark,
Wolves,
Beware,
Then out they jump,
With a leap and a slosh,
The predator's dead.

**Jennifer Ingram (12)**
**Bay House School, Gosport**

# Dawn Of The Dead

In the Gosport graveyard, zombies awake,
And come to attack, led by Satan.
They are coming to get you when you are asleep,
They are coming to eat and eat.
They don't want pizza, they don't want a shoe,
They are coming after you!

A new mayor has been chosen,
Because the last one has gone,
He disappeared at dawn.

Then a tank comes along,
And starts shooting all day long.
Blowing their heads off all through the night,
But they are still alight,
They haven't died; that is a fright.

Attacking the people all through the night.

It is the dawn of the dead,
Get it into your head.

*Bang!*

**Jake Harber  (12)**
**Bay House School, Gosport**


# Winter

The winter has fallen,
The air is so cold.
The plants do not grow,
And the mammals store food.
They hibernate too so they can keep warm,
And they do not come out, till winter has gone.

**Max Rumsey  (11)**
**Bay House School, Gosport**

# Puppies

Puppies are not just for Christmas,
Trust me I know this much,
They need to be loved and often hugged,
You play with them,
You stay with them,
And train them to do tricks,
Or make them go fetch sticks,
But most of all you need to want them.

If you do not want them do not buy them,
Do not abuse them or they will cry, whimper and sob,
You'll be sacked from the job of looking after one,
You'll have guts to go out in the sun.

You need to feed them and give them plenty to drink,
Before you buy you'd better think,
What does it need? You know, a collar and toys,
Make sure you know if it's a girl or a boy.

Take them for walks twice a day,
If they've got their jab (I forgot to say,)
Pay the vet if they get sick,
Oh and I forgot to mention if,
They are lonely buy them a friend,
Or take them to the park again and again.

**Joanna Sadler  (11)**
**Bay House School, Gosport**

# Twinkle Toes

The other day I saw a bear sitting on my bed,
He was crying and I could see he had a cut upon his head.
I sat by him and held his hand while saying, 'What's up with you?'
He then said 'I'm a sad bear who doesn't know what to do.
I'm a big fat clumsy bum,
Who is really, really dumb.'
'Oh don't cry,' I said to him, 'I am clumsy too.'
Then I gave him a *huge* hug.
'What's your name?' I said to him, he replied with a shrug,
'Twinkle Toes I'll call you, because you have brightened up my day.'
Then he shouted, '*Oh my goodness,* I've got to get away.'
'Oh what a shame,
I might not ever see you again.'
He gave me one last look then completely vanished,
Rumble went my stomach, I was completely famished.
I went to the kitchen to get some lunch,
Then gobbled it down *munch, munch, munch.*
Before I noticed a package on the table,
Whose was it? It had no label,
I opened it up and looked inside,
At that moment I could have cried,
It was a teddy bear addressed to me,
Twinkle Toes I called it.

**Cathy Brace  (11)**
**Bay House School, Gosport**

# Dinosaur Rampage

On an island south of Brazil,
Many species of dinosaur closed in for the kill.
Thought to be dead,
Lived and bred.

The arena stood there all ready to go,
The dinosaurs charged to get the front row.
Thought to be dead,
Lived and bred.

The first dinosaur in the ring posed like an actor,
The crowd cheered as it was a raptor.
Thought to be dead,
Lived and bred.

Behind the crowd an alien figure,
Let out a loud and raucous snigger.
Thought to be dead,
Lived and bred.

A sleeping adult on the floor,
Woke up and let out a mighty roar.
Thought to be dead,
Lived and bred.

'Hang on,' the thing cried, 'I smell a rat,'
The dino charged and the thing went splat.
Thought to be dead,
Lived and bred.

**Adam Pym  (11)**
**Bay House School, Gosport**

# Opposite

Come here children, sit on the floor,
And hear a story never told before.
Now I will tell you about a world you did not know existed,
And on the charts it is not listed.
You will not find this planet in the Milky Way,
Because it is two million miles away.
I had to hitch-hike a space bus to get there,
So I jumped on the back without paying the fare.
It took a day and a half on the bus,
I had to be silent without making a fuss.
When I had reached my destination,
I got off and saw a sign saying planet inflation.
What was weird was the people spoke in fluent Earth words,
And in the sky were big ugly birds.
They were bigger than the people, I thought they were on drugs,
They looked like a mob of gangsters and thugs.
This world was totally different to people from Earth,
Trees upside down and men giving birth.
The females were large, much taller than earthlings,
With flaps of skin that looked something like bat wings.
I looked at a house and saw it winking,
And they were alive smiling and speaking!
I was confused and my head was spinning,
But little did I know this was only the beginning.
Then I saw a squirrel that looked harmless,
But then it showed its teeth and it tried to make me armless!
So I ran and ran through this opposite land, I needed some
                                        help, I wanted a hand!
No one would help me, but then I found a bus,
And with it I got back to people like us!

**Elliot Samphier  (12)**
**Bay House School, Gosport**

# Seasons - Haikus

All seasons are great,
Each in their own special way,
Filled with excitement.

First comes cold winter,
Cherry noses all around,
Snow falls down softly.

New life sprouts so soon,
As Santa is forgotten,
Flowers start to bloom.

Adults relaxing,
Children screaming for ice cream,
In the boiling sun.

Summer is over,
As the leaves fall off most trees,
Back to hats and gloves.

They are the seasons,
So now it all starts again,
All seasons are great!

**Ciara McNamee  (11)**
**Bay House School, Gosport**

# Poisoned Love

She's going out the door and there's nothing to save me
She's really leaving me and there's nothing to save me,
Resounding on and on and on and on and,
Can't believe she's gone now there's no one to love me,
Gone for someone else and she's gone with the esprit,
Just driving off and off and off and off and,
She really did leave,
I wear this on my sleeve,
I only lost, I did not retrieve.

You gave me all your poison,
You gave me all your pills,
You gave me all your hopeless hearts and made me ill,
You're running after something that you'll never kill,
If this is what you want then fire at will.

The memories will pass and they'll never be open,
But I cannot forget the times when you had spoken,
On and on and on and on and,
I'm trying to forget and yet I remember,
The time that you had done it at the end of December,
Resounding on and on and on and on and,
She really did leave,
I wear this on my sleeve,
I only lost, I did not retrieve.

You gave me all your poison,
You gave me all your pills,
You gave me all your hopeless hearts and made me ill,
You're running after something that you'll never kill,
If this is what you want then fire at will.

**Christopher Nicholas  (12)**
**Bay House School, Gosport**

# My Destination

As I gallop round the field,
I feel the blowing wind,
My mane and tail are whipping wildly,
Jumping over hills,
I pass the sleeping dog,
As I run for freedom,
I run like the wind to reach my destination.

The stables are getting busier,
As the sun comes up,
The horses are being ridden,
Just cantering round and round,
The sweet smell of hay fills the air,
The clip-clop of the horse's shoes hits the ground,
They are coming to get me with a saddle in their hands,
I am going to be ridden,
Far away.

They saddle me up and take me away,
A little girl mounts me,
She pushes me into canter,
Without warming me up,
We ride to the hills,
Where I give a little buck,
The girl dismounts and gives me a hug,
Then whispers in my ear very softly,
'This is our destination.'

**Lucinda Needham  (11)**
**Bay House School, Gosport**

# My Panda

As white as a feather,
Feels just like leather,
She is a black moonlight,
She is awake nearly every night.

She has ears like rats,
Also, she has eyes just like bats,
You better beware,
She gives you an evil glare.

She sits there all day doing nothing,
She drags behind like an elephant,
She is almost as big as an armchair,
It's not a very good idea to have as a pet,
It will eat you I bet.

She walks on four legs,
Like most other animals,
My panda isn't a normal panda,
It is my cuddly panda,
Although she sounds like one,
*She isn't!*
She acts like a normal pet,
But she's only a toy.

**Loretta Harcombe  (11)**
**Bay House School, Gosport**

# Hallowe'en

The night is unnaturally cold,
Pumpkins are set on the doorstep,
Graves and trees are covered in mould,
Children in costumes are collecting chocolate and jelly beans,
Tonight is Hallowe'en.

From a patch of earth beneath a grave,
A hand shoots up, next the body tumbles out,
Blood, flesh and life are what the dead crave,
This night they will be seen,
Tonight is Hallowe'en.

They stumble through the houses,
Bulging eyes and bare feet,
Wearing torn clothes, their shirts covered in louses,
Their skin is rotten and green,
Tonight is Hallowe'en.

They grab their first victim, an elderly man,
They rip his skin and eat his soul,
Then walk north across the land,
Every one of them, the stout, the disfigured, the lean,
Go back to their graves, it is the end of Hallowe'en.

**Cora Morrissey  (12)**
**Bay House School, Gosport**

# The Boogie Monster

When I'm in bed tucked up warm and tight,
And the outside sky is filled up with the night,
I just close my eyes when something goes *bump!*
Then a shadow is formed of a great big lump,
And this is what it said.

'I'm a boogie woogie monster
I'm here to have a dance,
So if you want to have some fun, this is your chance,
A booga looga dooga wooga aba daba doo!'

Next night when I was sleeping,
My eyes were slightly peeping,
Then I saw the dancing lump,
As it did a twirly jump,
And this is what it said.

'I'm a boogie woogie monster,
I'm here to have a dance,
So if you want some fun, this is your chance,
A booga looga dooga wooga aba daba doo!'

**Lauren Nicoll  (11)**
**Bay House School, Gosport**

# In The Old Haunted House

In the old haunted house beware of the ghosts,
They swoop around like wisps of smoke.
You will hear the howling of the wind in the trees,
And the jangling of old rusty keys.
In the old haunted house beware of the ghosts,
They swoop around like wisps of smoke.
You will smell the rotten food from the kitchen,
And the scent of mouldy cheese.
In the old haunted house beware of the ghosts,
They swoop around like wisps of smoke.
You will see the boarded up windows,
And the picture of an old black widow.
In the old haunted house beware of the ghosts
They swoop around like wisps of smoke.
You will feel the musty air on your face,
And the dust in an empty space.
In the old haunted house beware of the ghosts,
They swoop around like wisps of smoke.
You will taste the presence of long-dead spirits,
And the taste of prehistoric people.
So, your best bet is to stay away,
For the house is clearly haunted,
So do not be taunted to go near the house,
For it could mean life or death!

**Victoria Dale  (11)**
**Bay House School, Gosport**

# Look

Look at the leaves swirling around,
Having no care to touch the ground.
Look at the fish playing together,
I wonder what it's like to play whatever the weather.
Look at the babies rolling on the floor,
I remember shouting 'More, more, more!'
Look at the flowers smelling sweet,
With so much detail pretty and petite.
Look at the birdies flying up high,
I wish I could be one and touch the sky.
Look at the sun, hot as fire,
Everyone knows it's what we desire.
Look at the sea calm and quiet,
Everyone knows it can cause a riot.
Look at those people who are so vain,
Never thinking of others to whom they cause pain.
Look at the glitter sparkling bright,
I bet that could light up an orphan's night.
Look at the food in that store,
People wanting more and more.
Look at yourself in the mirror hall,
And think of yourself lucky all in all.
Look at the animals being killed forever,
When will it stop? Probably never.
Look at that man planting trees,
Helping the poor breathe in breeze.
Look at your things and stare for a while,
For your happiness people will go a mile.
Look at the stars and then you'll see,
Just how beautiful the world can be.

**Paige Nolan  (12)**
**Bay House School, Gosport**

# Our World

The world is a special place,
With a lot of spare space.
There was a man who planted trees,
Planted acorns while on his knees.
The man realized his world was dying,
Which meant that every day he felt like crying.
He gave us his life's worth trust,
So look after the world, he did, we must!

The world is a special place,
With a lot of spare space,
There was a man who built our houses,
He got rid of our rats and mouses.
The man realized there were homeless people,
Lucky ones lived in a steeple.
He gave us his life's trust,
So look after the world, he did, we must.

The world is a special place,
With a lot of spare space.
There was a person who puts us together,
Treasured us forever and ever and ever.
Spent days and days putting us together,
Get rid of us? No! Not ever.
They gave us their life's worth trust,
Of course they exist, they made us!

**Courtney Bailey (11)**
**Bay House School, Gosport**

# Rainbow

Red for a heart,
Red for a book.
Yellow for the sun,
Yellow for the beach.
Pink for a face,
Pink for a rose.
Green for grass,
Green for a frog.
Purple for a dress,
Purple for flowers.
Orange for a pumpkin,
Orange for an orange.
Blue for the sea,
Blue for the sky.
Red,
Yellow,
Pink,
Green,
Purple,
Orange and,
Blue.
Rainbows are magic,
A sight to see.
It will fill you with joy,
Never make you cry,
Brightness everywhere,
Over the hills and far away,
With its magic so strong,
Sparkle everywhere,
I love rainbows and as you can see,
Rainbows are magic and will always be!

**Georgina-Emily Cook  (11)**
**Bay House School, Gosport**

# I Give You A Kiss

I give you a kiss,
All warm and tender.
All pink and shiny round your lips,
Welcoming you home from a hard day.

I give you a kiss,
So nice and sweet.
Making you feel better,
When you come home from work.

I give you a kiss,
So pleased and lovable.
When saying thank you,
From something that's happened.

I give you a kiss,
Calm and gentle.
Just after having tea,
Now I must go to work with the kiss left on me.

**Madison Taylor (11)**
**Bay House School, Gosport**

# Conker

I give you a conker,
It's as round as a ball, and as brown as a bear.

I give you a conker,
It's as small as a mouse, and as shiny as a penny.

I give you a conker,
It reflects like a mirror, and it smells like brown sauce,

I give you a conker,
It feels like a stone, but is as smooth as babies' skin,

I give you a conker,
It's as slippy as a fish, and sounds like a giant walking around,

I give you a conker,
It has lines like ripples in the ocean, and has a top like
melted chocolate.

I give you a conker,
When it falls off the tree, it sounds like a firework exploding.

Here is my conker.

**Lucy Howell  (12)**
**Bay House School, Gosport**

# Star Rider

I'm riding the back of a silver light,
Gliding towards the moon.
Gazing back down to the fallen star,
That once used to be my home.

The wild wind whispers in my ear,
As night's shadow closes in.
And far beyond the golden galaxy,
I hear the sound of the marmen,
Lying in wait for me.

Their eyes are ferocious flames of fire,
Burning into my soul.
Their hands are the ghosts of deadly spiders,
Moving in for the kill.
Their silver skin casts an eerie light,
That cuts through the darkness of the charcoal night.
These are the men from the mountains of Mars.

**Hermione Cameron  (12)**
**Bedgebury School, Goudhurst**


# The Year 3000

It's the year 3000,
There's no more war.
No more fighting,
Everyone is hand in hand.

It's the year 3000,
There's no more poverty.
Everyone has enough food and extra,
No one's dying from starvation.

But this is all a dream,
There might still be war and fighting.
Poverty and hunger,
But maybe it will all be safe and happy,
Who knows until then?

**Katie Wooding Jones  (12)**
**Bedgebury School, Goudhurst**

# Who Knows Where I'll Be

The time is now two minutes to six,
A minute ago was the past,
A minute ahead is the future.

The time now is one minute to six,
At five o'clock, I watched TV,
At six o'clock, I'll have my tea.

The time now is six o'clock,
At seven o'clock Mum will say, 'Get ready for bed,'
At eight o'clock, she'll repeat what she said.

Tomorrow I might be at school.

Next week I might be at home.

Next month I might be on a plane.

Next year I'll be a *whole year older!*
In five years' time I might be making the most important
                                        choice in my life,

In ten years' time who knows where I'll be!

I'll live my life to the fullest and live each day like the last.

**Eva Tang  (12)**
**Bedgebury School, Goudhurst**

# Dreams

How old are you now 1, 2 or 3?
What do you dream of?
What do you see?

Do you dream of cats, dogs and mice
Or to travel the world, not once but twice?
Do you want to be a sailor and live on a ship
Or become a waitress and get a good tip?
Want to have a mansion, cottage or a flat
And furnish it from top to toe, from curtains to the mat?
Will you have children? Little rascals they are!
But make sure where they live is well above par!
Where will you live, Germany, France, Spain,
Or will you stay in England?
That's only if you don't mind a little drop of rain.
Will you get to see humans on Mars?
Will you take part, and stare into the stars?

I can tell you more than one thousand things,
But I can't tell you what your future brings.
Because only you know,
Where you will go!

**Abi Firth (12)**
**Bedgebury School, Goudhurst**

# The Future

What does the future hold?
Is it a story just untold?
Is it a mere fairy tale
Or is it as insignificant as a snail?

Will everything be free tomorrow
Or will we still have to borrow?
Will we ever find out
What life is all about?

What will people wear, what will people eat?
Will they still have hair or will they have webbed feet?
Will they learn to fly high up in the sky,
Or live beneath the sea in watery harmony?

We might never know,
The world could glow.
We will have to wait and see,
What the world will be.

**Kayleigh Gowen-Smith  (14)**
**Bedgebury School, Goudhurst**

# Bullying Is Like . . .

A one-way fight,
A big, harsh bite,
A dog barking every minute, every hour,
Being pinpointed down by the army,
A lifetime of bad memories,
Dreading the day all over again,
Getting ready for a fight you just can't win.

**Calum Georgiou  (12)**
**Hartsdown Technology College, Margate**

# The Song Of The Dolphin

I'm the Formula 1 racing car,
I'm a silver shooting star.

I'm the king of the sea,
No one has ever seen someone as fast as me.

I'm the cheetah of the ocean,
I'm full of motion.

I'm the shiny sun,
I'm the bullet in a gun.

I'm the icing on the cake,
My sea is the big lake.

I'm big and strong,
I'm very long.

I can swim but I can't run,
I'm the athlete when the race is won.

**Aysha Begum  (13)**
**Hartsdown Technology College, Margate**

# Bullying Is Like . . .

A never-ending horror film,
A never-ending black hole,
A prison cell,
Being a ghost,
A never-ending black cloud,
A never-ending row,
A monster permanently in your head.

**Laura Hodges  (12)**
**Hartsdown Technology College, Margate**

# The Song Of A Cat

I am a ginger cake,
I'm never awake.

I'm a real winner,
And a sinner.

I'm the Pied Piper,
I'm a rat-killing sniper.

I'm a fluffy cloud,
I'm a microphone that's loud.

I'm a speeding athlete,
When I play I cheat.

I am slow and graceful,
I can carry a case full.

I'm a beautiful vision,
I'm an animal calculator, adding and dividing.

**Hannah Kerrigan  (14)**
**Hartsdown Technology College, Margate**


# Bullying Is Like . . .

Committing a crime,
A black hole never ending,
Someone stabbing you in the heart,
A car driven to the limits,
Having a brick smashed in your face,
Being trapped in a dark corner,
Falling down a never-ending hole.

**Fraser Lawrance  (13)**
**Hartsdown Technology College, Margate**

# The Door

A realm into the future,
Looking into me.
A blank slate,
Starting out fresh, a new day, a new day.
Pushing against its warmth and softness,
Wraps around my body.
Feelings of hope, desires for wealth and enjoyment come with me,
Sharp intake of breath,
As a fear of death poisons this moment,
I push onwards into blackness.

Light-headedness overcomes me,
Iodine fills my nose,
Chattering and muttering hurts my ears,
Bright light strains my eyes,
Every hope and fear is laid on me,
May I be the best I can be,
As I begin to wait.

**Matthew Brown  (15)**
**Hartsdown Technology College, Margate**

# Bullying Is Like . . .

A one-way street,
You can never win or lose,
You're a prisoner,
You wake up the next day,
Wishing it would go away,
It's like a virus you can't get rid of,
Maybe one day they will find a cure.

**Tony Handley  (12)**
**Hartsdown Technology College, Margate**

# War Poem

Just imagine you and the fearsome men,
Out here on the field like in a game of rugby.
Two halves ducking and diving,
To be shot in the end.
A game of control and strategy,
To take on the enemy.
All it takes is one wrong move,
And the opponent's trigger will be pushed.
As you cry for help,
With a hole in your chest.
You stagger to safety,
A drunken man tripping in to his own bed.
You may go to war with your country but you are on your own,
Like a stray sheep on a mountain peak.

**Luke Alexander (14)**
**Hartsdown Technology College, Margate**


# War Poem

Blood and mud mingled,
We are fighting back.
Enemy advancing,
Back frothing blood.
They stop moving,
We start advancing.

Bodies decomposing,
Stench of skunks.
Skeletons lie everywhere,
Sinking in the mud.
Mortars firing,
The water mixed with blood.

**Robert Payn (13)**
**Hartsdown Technology College, Margate**

# Dark Eyes In The Night

Dark eyes in the night,
Bright eyes that search for prey,
Eyes like glowing diamonds,
Sparkling eyes that guide his way.

What will he find?
What will he do?
He might just find a creepy clue.

He is big and furry,
And scary too,
We never know quite what he'll do.

He goes out hunting every night,
He might just give you a nasty fright,
The sun is rising; time to go home,

I might see you again; you never know.

**Amelia Acaster  (12)**
**Hartsdown Technology College, Margate**

# The Vampire!

As the night slowly gets darker,
The vampires are starting to rise,
And they have this sudden urge to eat,
So they transform into bats and hunt for blood.

As they hunt their senses get stronger,
And then they spot their first victim,
So as they swoop down for their first kill,
Their thirst for blood gets stronger.

But when they finally reach their victim,
They see some rays reflecting off the windows,
So they leave their victim and go back to their coffins,
They think to themselves, the night was a disappointment.

And the victim's life was spared.

**Matt Leighton  (15)**
**Hartsdown Technology College, Margate**

# The Seven Stages Of Me

*(Inspired by 'As You Like It')*

The seven stages of me,
From the start to the end of my life.
My person changing,
Yet staying the same.
At first in the cradle, with smooth pale skin.
In her mother's arms with loving care,
Yet giving unwanted gifts!
And then, first steps, first words,
Her parents' pride and joy.
First hairs on head, a cute toddler,
But to siblings, a blockage to their parents' attention!
Long hair tied back in plaits,
Photographs in her first school uniform,
Trudging unwillingly to school,
In her eyes, an unnecessary place.
High heels, short skirts, constant nagging from parents,
Arriving into teenage-hood.
What used to be an annoying boy is now the only one.
Big steps to maturity and now has found a man,
White dress, flowers and veil, walking up the aisle.
Happy memories, possession of both a ring,
And a newborn, sleeping soundly in the cot.
And then the next and final steps into a grandparent's world,
Grey hair and walking stick,
But then into an eternal grave.

**Katherine Lowe  (11)**
**Hartsdown Technology College, Margate**

# Bullying Is Like . . .

A storm ahead,
I'm only safe when I'm asleep in bed,
My dreams are like torture,
But real life is worse.

**Rebecca Rhodes  (13)**
**Hartsdown Technology College, Margate**

# The Song Of A Lion

I'm a runner like a hummer,
I'm the power of a flower.

I'm a fierce hunt,
I'm not a little runt.

I'm a burning fire,
In my heart's desire.

I'm a smooth beat,
I don't crack under heat.

I'm part of a pack,
I'm the king not the jack.

I'm here to stay,
I'm not easily pushed away.

I'm cute and cuddly,
But under I'm hot and bubbly.

I'm nearly extinct,
So just stop and think!

**Kyle Gleeson  (13)**
**Hartsdown Technology College, Margate**


# A Door

As I journey towards this door,
I reach out and touch,
My body saturated,
I push against it and feel it pull me through,
I am in nothing and then bathed in light,
I open my eyes,
My world begins . . .

**Remy Glendinning  (13)**
**Hartsdown Technology College, Margate**

# Season - Haiku

Leaves of brown, orange
And red scattered on the floor,
Shiny conkers smash.

Footprints in the snow,
The crystal-white winter ice,
The sparkling sunshine.

Pink blossom floating,
Like soft skin. Newborn spring lambs,
Frolic in meadows.

Glazing sun shining,
Through my bedroom windowpane,
Football in the park.

**Matthew Reed (12)**
**Hartsdown Technology College, Margate**


# War Poem

My blood mingles with sweat and tears,
As the dead lie down in this rotting stench,
A soldier fighting like a deadly machine,
People dying, falling every minute.

The trenches are getting smaller and smaller,
As soldiers are screaming and being tortured,
As the air becomes dark and black,
Bombs fly all about.

**Miranda Spencer (14)**
**Hartsdown Technology College, Margate**

# The Song Of A Butterfly

I'm a flashing rainbow,
I'm a bow and arrow.

I'm a dancing beam of sunlight,
I'm a little silver knight.

I'm a fairy cake,
I give, I don't take.

I'm a fragile parcel,
I'm queen of the castle.

I'm a lonely old man,
I'm a multicoloured van.

I'm a fast motorbike,
I'm a silly trike.

I've got the power of a flower.

**Amy McGregor (13)**
**Hartsdown Technology College, Margate**


# War Poem

The rotted smell of skeletal beings,
The visions of the trenches,
Walking through the dungeons of evil,
The sadness,
The crying,
Seeing your best mate dying,
The destructive bombs blasting,
The blood puddles everywhere,
And somewhere death is about to appear.

**Laura Cheshire (13)**
**Hartsdown Technology College, Margate**

# Bullying

His hand zipped through the air,
His hand pulled my hair,
I kicked and screamed,
In my face he beamed,
He strangled me, I got out of breath,
I panicked, I thought I was close to death.

In came Sir around the corner,
My face was hot, it felt like a sauna,
The bully ran away,
This happened again the very next day.

**Daniel Pellegrini (12)**
**Hartsdown Technology College, Margate**


# Bullying Is Like . . .

A bull charging at you,
A cat clawing you,
A dead body hanging over you,
A horse stamping on you,
A leopard tearing you apart,
An elephant stamping over you,
Being hidden away.

**Chloe McAteer (12)**
**Hartsdown Technology College, Margate**


# Bullying Is Like . . .

Bullying is like getting hit by a bike,
Being shot through the heart,
Needles being poked through you,
Being drowned in the sea,
Being hung on the wall,
Being trapped in prison.

**Eloise McGinley (12)**
**Hartsdown Technology College, Margate**

# Bullying Is Like . . .

Going to Hell,
Time never moving,
Being held hostage,
You're never alone,
Being close to death,
Being poked with knives,
A storm always with you,
A black cloud never floating away.

**Natalie Culver (12)**
**Hartsdown Technology College, Margate**


# Bullying

Bullying is when people go against you,
When people don't accept you,
When they disrespect day after day,
When they reject you like an old toy,
When they hurt you for who you are,
When they get you when you're alone,
When you feel that you're unknown.

**James Bartlett-Smith (12)**
**Hartsdown Technology College, Margate**


# Bullying Is Like . . .

Punches thrown like a trombone,
Horrible language repeated again and again,
You feel like running away,
No one cares.

**Daniel Utteridge (13)**
**Hartsdown Technology College, Margate**

# Bullying Is Like . . .

Being trapped in a prison and no one can free you,
Sharp pains pushed into your body and it doesn't matter how
                              hard you try, the pain remains,
Being surrounded by a black mist and you can't escape,
Being the only one alive and no one can hear you scream,
Being trapped in a bubble and no matter how much you prod
                              and poke, you're stuck.

**Rebecca Bedford  (12)**
**Hartsdown Technology College, Margate**


# Bullying Is Like . . .

Hell and it makes you feel like you're at the bottom of a well,
A bomb and it makes you feel wrong.

A ball of wool unravelling until you disappear,
You're constantly fighting the emotional jeers.

**Brandon Palmer  (12)**
**Hartsdown Technology College, Margate**


# Bullying Is Like . . .

Being stabbed in the heart,
Weapons are there wherever you turn,
A long journey far from over,
There's never a light at the end of the tunnel.

**Lauren Chapman  (13)**
**Hartsdown Technology College, Margate**

# The Song Of The Dog

I'm a slave, I'm a servant, and crimes I will prevent.

I'm a cop, I'm a searcher,
I'm the number one lurcher.

I'm a mountain, I'm a flea,
I'm as nimble as a bee.

I'm a bad boy, I'm a boff,
I'm that depressed-looking goth.

I'm the sun, I'm the moon,
I'm the cool kid or I'm the loon.

**Daniel Cass  (13)**
**Hartsdown Technology College, Margate**


# Bullying Is Like . . .

Someone stabbing your heart,
Being pushed through the dark,
Being trapped in a room,
Someone screaming 'Boo,'
You're always on the run,
You can't have any fun,
Never going out to play,
Your life is fading away.

**Lucy Gower  (12)**
**Hartsdown Technology College, Margate**

# The Seasons Of The Year

Spring, summer, autumn, winter,
Make the seasons of the year,
Some are hot, some are cold,
Some are never told!

At spring our long journey does begin,
When the snowflakes start to thin,
A daffodil is growing,
And all those shining blue rivers are flowing,
And newborn lambs always knowing,
That spring is its name!

Next comes the season of the sun,
Play on the beaches, have some fun,
Go on holiday - like to Spain,
Where gloves and scarves are a pain,
And summer is its name!

Soon the chill blows in,
And crowded beaches start to thin,
All the blossom trees are bare,
And nesting creatures start to stare,
From the autumn lair!

Soon the snowflakes start to fall,
On the mossy garden wall,
And people celebrate Christmas Day,
When Jesus was born they say,
In a manger he did lay,
And winter is its name!

**Izzy Worrall  (11)**
**Highcliffe School, Christchurch**

# My Friends

My friends are the best,
Some of us hate lemon zest,
We're friends together,
And will be forever,

I like Naomi most,
She lives near the coast,
I like Grace least,
'Cause when she's angry she's a beast.

Alex has black hair,
And likes to be fair,
Steff loves horses,
But hates subordinate clauses.

Olivia does karate,
And she likes a good party,
Danielle is pretty,
And loves shopping in the city.

I'm Elaine,
Some people make jokes that I'm a pain,
So that's why they're all my mates,
And we meet inside the school gates.

**Elaine Bell  (11)**
**Highcliffe School, Christchurch**

# How To Be A Friend

I am of course a loyal friend,
Who's there for everyone,
I play with them and sit with them,
And make sure they're having fun.

I invite them round my house for tea,
We giggle madly like clowns,
And then we sit down after all,
And make ourselves some crowns.

We make ourselves a midnight feast,
Like a little tea party,
We sit there stuffing our mouths with food,
And then we talk about me.

We then decide to get some sleep,
And we brush our teeth first,
We read a book then turn off the light,
And dream of being a nurse.

In the morning we yawn and stretch,
And get ourselves dressed,
My friend's mum comes to collect her,
And then I have a rest.

**Chloe Bentall (12)**
**Highcliffe School, Christchurch**


# Love

My grandma has lived for sixty-five years
She has known joy, sorrow and a few tears
Gran was born in Scotland; the land of Robert Burns
His poems she delights in, especially their twists and turns
His songs are romantic and so is his prose
And to finish I have to say
My love for her is like a red, red rose.

**Hannah Elkins (11)**
**Highcliffe School, Christchurch**

# Ballad Of The Lonely Guy

When you came home from school today,
Was he by the gate again?
Was he shaking by the rail?
The boy who was stuck halfway to Hell.

Was he sad? Was he fine?
The poor old kid from number nine,
His only friend is his alien John,
I don't believe him, I think he's wrong.

He's slightly bad, and naughty too,
He likes to smoke near us too,
He likes to swear, he thinks it's cool,
I don't think so, he's just a fool.

When you came home from school today,
Was he by the gate again?
I thought he had moved away,
But we'll never know, he didn't say!

**Robin Joynson  (11)**
**Highcliffe School, Christchurch**


# Friends

Everyone,
Yes everyone,
Needs friends!

They help you when you're in trouble,
They make you happy when you're sad,
They care for you,
Laugh and play too,
Yes they certainly do!

You see that friends are needed,
For you and for me,
Oh everyone,
Yes everyone,
Needs *friends!*

**Madeleine Daley-Brown  (11)**
**Highcliffe School, Christchurch**

# Friends

What is a friend?
A friend is someone who is great,
A special person, a best mate,
I didn't meet you by chance,
It must have been fate,
Someone who helps me through my fear,
Someone close and always near,
Someone for who I really care,
To laugh, have fun and always share,
Someone who's always in my heart,
Always together and never apart,
I'm never alone when we're together,
You'll always be my best friend forever!

**Rachel Baker  (11)**
**Highcliffe School, Christchurch**


# Hillsborough Disaster

One day there was a disaster
I didn't tell my master
I knew he wouldn't care
Because he's a bear
He always hits me
Until I need a pee
I sit in the toilet all day
Making sure I don't get in his way
Now this is why I'm talking to you
Because of the people who . . .
Died in a disaster
But I wish it was my master
They were squashed to death
Like my dear, sweet Beth
It was about '96
When I was holding bricks
It was a terrible disaster
Like what this second happened to my master.

**Jack Downs  (12)**
**Portchester School, Bournemouth**

# The Twin Towers

Osama bin Laden lay in wait,
To destroy America he would try,
But he attacked an innocent place,
And made too many people cry,
They all died because of one foolish man.

September the eleventh, a normal day,
Yet many did not live to tell,
The NY Trade Center was the place,
Where on Earth there appeared a hell,
They all died because of one foolish man.

The planes struck around midday,
Killing most inside,
Osama said it wasn't him,
Yet many know he lied,
They all died because of one foolish man.

Children lost their parents,
Husbands lost their wives,
Many, too sad to take the pain,
Decided to take their lives,
They all died because of one foolish man.

Nothing can affect the memory,
Nothing can affect the love,
But they all live in the knowledge,
They are up in the heavens above,
They all died because of one foolish man.

**Rowan Lee  (12)**
**Portchester School, Bournemouth**

# Old Trafford Disaster

Manchester United and Arsenal were rivals,
The Old Trafford stadium collapsed,
The fans went down in piles,
A bit like in single files,
Three people died.

The ref blew the whistle,
The fans were throwing missiles,
'Look Ref, there's missiles,' said Jose Antonio Reyes,
The first boy who died was a Spanish boy called Treyes,
Another three people died.

The goalkeeper kicked the ball high,
The ball hit a bird which died,
You could see things spinning around,
They were hands,
There were 67,031 fans,
Another three people died.

Arsenal scored the first goal, it was Ljungburg,
1-0 to Arsenal, Man Utd fans were booing, *boo, boo.*
They say it was the last game in May,
They were pushing and shoving,
Another three people died.

It was the end of the match,
The three points were snatched,
Arsenal were victorious, winning the Premiership title,
They were still throwing missiles,
Another three people died.

**Jamie Kascioglu  (12)**
**Portchester School, Bournemouth**

# The Crash Of All Dreams

There was a car crash one day,
The owner had a lot to pay,
He lost his wife,
Risked his life,
Just to see if the car was OK.

There was a car crash one day,
The owner had a lot to say,
He broke his arm,
He looked so calm,
Just to see if the car was OK.

There was a car crash one day,
It was in the month of May,
The owner lost his memory,
Just to see his wife in a cemetery,
Just to see if the car was OK.

There was a car crash one day,
The owner was delivering a bale of hay,
He was unconscious,
The car was monstrous,
Just to see if the car was OK.

There was a car crash one day,
It was the owner's birthday,
It was the 23rd,
He was singing like a bird,
Just to see if the car was OK.

**Bradley Wilson  (12)**
**Portchester School, Bournemouth**

# Jack Frost

My name is Jack
And my neighbours I just can't hack
I hate my mum and my dad
They think I'm bad
I'm just hyper
My sister wears a diaper.

I went for a long walk
And never came back
Because the snow and weather I couldn't hack
I froze to death
My last thoughts were of Beth
My girlfriend.

I started to die
And before dying I started crying
My toes fell off
Nibbled by a moth.

I wasn't found till spring
My parents didn't care
My girlfriend moved on
Now I'm a myth and forgotten like a bomb
I'm back to wreak havoc
Don't forget to wear a glove
Because if you don't, I will come from above.

**Connor Daly  (12)**
**Portchester School, Bournemouth**

# School Day

It's a school day today,
And the weekend's time to go away,
I have to learn English and maths,
I've got a test, so I hope I pass!
My English teacher moans and groans,
And gives us a lecture about mobile phones.
At lunch a boy gives me a right old smacking
And Mr Bradey sends him packing.
It's last lesson now,
Oh, how I pray,
The weekend is only four days away.
I hope I have a nice old tutor,
Instead I get a lesson on how to make pewter.
I've had enough,
I'm leaving now,
Someone's got a detention
For calling the teacher a silly old cow.

**Zachary Bradley (12)**
**Portchester School, Bournemouth**


# Gone And Passed

All those laughs, all was done,
Your beautiful smile, as gleaming as the sun.

It happened in your sleep, why did you let go?
After you went, my heart sank so low.

Now that you have gone and passed,
The clearest memory is you through a glass.

I know you wouldn't like to see me sad,
But I'm writing this with memories we shared and had.

Even though it's been so long,
I still can't believe that you're gone.

You'll know I sent those tears up to Heaven,
But as you know, the pain's been done.

**James Keith (15)**
**Portchester School, Bournemouth**

# The Boy And His Poem

There was a boy sat in a classroom
And the teacher said, 'Write a poem.'
The boy hung his head
He wracked his brain for ideas,
But oh no! Writer's block!

The boy looked up at the clock,
Then down at his page.
Fifteen minutes and no words.
What can he do with no ideas?
He's completely stumped.

Thirty minutes passed, thirty minutes to go,
Ghouls, ghosts and goblins,
All have come and gone,
But still no words,
What can he do?

He looks up at the clock,
Fifty-five minutes have gone,
But no words have flowed.
One minute to go - still no words,
So he finally raises his hand
And in a trembling voice says,
'Can I give it to you tomorrow?'

**Michael Sauget  (15)**
**Portchester School, Bournemouth**


# The Zombies

D own in the wood on a dark, dark night
R acing a vampire, causing some fright
A long the path the zombies arose
C reeping along in their tattered clothes
U ndead and ghostly sounds all around
L eaving their graves as big holes in the ground
A ll you can hear is the eerie sound.

**Henry Ho-Yin Cheung  (12)**
**Portchester School, Bournemouth**

*Young Writers - POP! Southern England*

# Seasons

Summer, summer, it's not here for long,
Only a few months and it will be gone.
So rush to the beach and jump in the sea,
Imagine you're a butterfly, graceful and free.

Winter, winter, it seems like forever,
That's probably because of the cold and wet weather.
Look at the trees all frozen and strong,
Can you see the forest? It's an icy throng.

Spring, spring, it's a wonderful thing,
The newborn animals and flowers it brings.
Laughing children playing with ease,
The wind is blowing softly, it's only a breeze,

Autumn, autumn, is when yellow leaves fall,
Time to pack up the lemonade stall.
Brown leaves on the ground get old and decay,
Not much is happening on the first season day.

**Kelsey Bennett (12)**
**Portchester School, Bournemouth**

# Peer Pressure

They act like your friends, but somehow you know they're not.
They call round for you like they're your friends, but somehow you
know they're not.
They make you do stuff you don't want to because they're your
mates, but somehow you know they're not.
You smoke and get into fights because it's cool, according to your
mates, but somehow you know it's not.
You're in jail for vandalism and your friends don't write to you . . .
Now you know they're definitely not your friends!

**Callum Ford (15)**
**Portchester School, Bournemouth**

# Cauldron Troubles

In this cauldron you need to add,
Lots of chickens that are mad.
Kill a human and take out the heart,
Then pierce a human brain with a dart.
Take a skunk and put it in a jar,
Now fill up the cauldron with tar.

Bang, sizzle, burn and fry,
Never drink this or you will die.

Take a rabbit and turn it inside out,
This is going to be revolting without a doubt.
Rip out some eyeballs and mix them in,
Don't forget the garbage bin.
Pour in some thick blood,
Don't pour in too much or it will flood.

Bang, sizzle, burn and fry,
Never drink this or you will die.

Peel off and add in some werewolf skin,
Keep the layers nice and thin.
Cut off lots of fingers and human hair,
Also roast in parts of a huge bear.
Shake in the crushed flesh and bones,
Now it is gruesome enough for you to hear moans.

Bang, sizzle, burn and fry,
Now it is time for you to die!

**Muhammad Waqas Ahmad  (12)**
**Portchester School, Bournemouth**

# Changing Seasons

Trees swaying in the breeze,
Seasons pass with little ease.

Spring is a time that's full of bloom,
No need now for that dusty old broom.
Flowers make the fields stand out proud,
Bees are buzzing so very loud.
Trees are growing leaves once more,
Leaves are different colours, colours galore!

Summer is when the sun shines warm,
Now the weather is on form.
It's so hot now, they can make
Ice creams and lemonade,
These are things that people make.

It's autumn now, so many leaves,
This is what a garden receives.
It's also time for Hallowe'en,
That's enough to scare the Queen.
With a scream and a roar,
Children stand at the door.

Winter's here now, what a chill,
To see mountains of snow forming a hill.
Kids jump with joy, snow has come,
Dads all groan with a bottle of rum.
We all know it's Christmas time,
It's not a time for so much crime.

**Troy Stensel  (12)**
**Portchester School, Bournemouth**

# Four Seasons

Summer, autumn, winter and spring,
Those four words, don't they just give you a ring?
These four are called seasons, that we adore,
They can be next to you, maybe right at your door!

Summer is when the sun comes out to play,
Go on, come out and check out your local bay!
Sorry, but summer does not last very long,
But autumn's here, pressing your doorbell, *ding-dong!*
Autumn makes no difference, but still, let the shivering commence!

It's now time for joyous winter!
Let's now start to shake and quiver.
Ice and snow, we want more of that ice galore!
After a few months that ice will melt,
Now take off your coat, shirt, fur or felt!

Spring is the time when plants start to grow,
The wind blows the trees to and fro.
Well, those are the seasons a year will bring,
I bet the word 'seasons' will now give a ring!

**Felix Apalisok (13)**
**Portchester School, Bournemouth**


# Graveyard

Walking through the graveyard
With the rustling trees in your face,
It looks like you've been followed
And attacked by the unknown.
Their bloody flesh ripping out of the earth,
Grabbing the nearest thing to pull themselves out of the grave.
Not long until they're ripping out all over the earth,
Not long before they're all out!
These are the unknown!

**Charlie Cook (12)**
**Portchester School, Bournemouth**

# Heroes With Dirty Faces

The bells sound and down they come,
Pulling their fire gear on as they run.
Running to the red machine,
Just like in a child's dream.
As the bay doors open they speed off,
There is no time to cough.

The sirens switch on as they speed,
Lights start flashing in a plead.
'Get out of my way, I'm on a shout,'
Letting everybody know that they're about.
They speed through the red traffic lights,
As they go it makes quite a sight.

As they reach their destination,
They pull out the hoses to stop suffocation.
The water shoots out from the end of the pipe,
It douses the flames that are so ripe.
The rescue crew go in without showing fright,
When they bring someone out, it's such a delight.

Adrenalin rushing,
As everyone starts hushing.
When the fire goes out,
It is all thanks to the water spout.
And on the way back they smile with joy,
At saving yet another boy.

**Jon Packer  (12)**
**Portchester School, Bournemouth**

# Gothic

G hosts and ghouls creep around
O ver the hills and under the ground
T rees swaying from side to side
H aunted house to go and hide
I ncredible monster with two heads
C reeping spiders making their webs.

**Jason Everitt  (12)**
**Portchester School, Bournemouth**

# Should He Do It?

'Should I do it?' he asked himself,
Does he have a good reason?
Even though he has everlasting wealth,
Things hadn't gone well this season,
If he fell he would go to Hell.

He stood on top of a building,
He wondered if he had anything to live for.
A picture of his wife he was holding,
He had always wanted to go on a world tour,
If he fell he would go to Hell.

His wife had died a week ago
She died in a car accident.
In it he lost his toe
And his car got a big dent.
If he fell he would go to Hell.

He decided not to jump
But instead he slipped.
He fell into a garbage dump.
Too much alcohol he had sipped
He fell and went to Hell.

**Danny Supple  (13)**
**Portchester School, Bournemouth**


# Dracula

Black and spooky cobwebs flowing
White teeth flashing, candles burning
His red and black cape, spinning and turning
Darkness is falling, his face is looming
Prowling along the stairs as he goes creeping.

**Ben King  (12)**
**Portchester School, Bournemouth**

# At The End Of The Day

The man was driving
On the motorway
He wouldn't be driving
At the end of the day.

The man was in a car crash
On the motorway
The man had his car bashed
At the end of the day.

The man was in agony
On the motorway
He thought *what a tragedy*
At the end of the day.

The man had a broken leg
On the motorway
The man was bleeding from the head
At the end of the day.

The man was in the ambulance
On the motorway
He said, 'This day has been so turbulent,'
At the end of the day.

**Michael Robertson  (12)**
**Portchester School, Bournemouth**


# Romania

Cold, dark and mysterious,
As we lurk in Romania's sharp Pistol Mountains.
Gazing over us like dark gods watching us.
The mist is like a deserted graveyard
And the signs warn people off
Like a creature fighting off its prey.
The dark, windy path leading to a castle,
Creepy as the grave.

**Sergio La Mantia  (12)**
**Portchester School, Bournemouth**

# House Fire

There was a house fire,
On Drewly Lane,
There were screeches coming from the house next door,
Why does it happen to me?

There was a flickering of light,
I know them,
Or do I?
Why does it happen to me?

A siren came from the left,
I realised it was a fire engine,
*It was started by a lit cigarette.*
Why does it happen to me?

Oh, I heard some shouting,
'Oh, help me!'
It's my best friend. Help them?
Why does it happen to me?

I ran out of the house, shouting,
So wanting to help.
I was so upset,
Why does it happen to me?

They said I couldn't do anything,
I had a flashback of the past.
I was lying, sobbing on the ground.
Why does it happen to me?

There was nothing left of the house,
Only a few dusty ashes.
Rest in peace.
It's a waste of a good family.
Why does it happen to me?

**Sam Dargan (13)**
**Portchester School, Bournemouth**

# There Was A Ghost One Day

There was a ghost one day
I heard it
I saw it
I smelt it
I felt it.

There was a ghost one day
It was in my mind
In my car
In my house
In my room
In my bed.

There was a ghost one day in my room
I felt it shiver down my clothes and spine
I felt it near my bed, near me
I felt it next to me
Then I saw it.

There was a ghost one day
I've seen it
It looked like a white cloth
No eyes
No ears
No mouth
No nose
Just a white sheet of cloth.

There was a ghost one day
It was haunting me everywhere
In the shop
At home
In my car
*Everywhere!*

**Shahibur Rahman  (12)**
**Portchester School, Bournemouth**

# The Vampire

A vampire
A ghastly monster
It lurks in the scary darkness
It comes out to kill for a bride
It is there but it is gone
With one bite of its fangs
You will start your new life
As a vampire you will have eternal life
You bite for food
You kill for fun
You fly like a bat
You disappear in the fog
Teeth sharp as a sword
Your skin as white as paper.

**Joe Connor  (13)**
**Portchester School, Bournemouth**


# The Hunter

He comes out at night
When he sees the moonlight
Gives out a howl
When he goes on the prowl.

He hunts for meat
With the movement of his feet
He could rip you into shreds
Then he leaves you for dead.

Is he real?
We'll never know
Will we have to wait
Until he shows?

**William McDowell  (12)**
**Portchester School, Bournemouth**

# A Creep Doesn't Sleep

G hosts, werewolves and vampires,
O ther nights you need a lamp fire,
T hings that weep and things that creep,
H ell is a place where you can't sleep.
I n places like mansions and other places,
C astles have traps and if you get caught you'll lose your faces.

H orrible things like a witch,
O ther spells make you itch,
R eapers are scary,
R ight-hand touch and you'll die.
O nly vampires hate the cross,
R eady to bite. It's your loss.

**Thomas Caullay  (12)**
**Portchester School, Bournemouth**


# Hallowe'en

H owling wolves in the night
A nxious vampires ready to bite
L urking, silent ghosts haunt
L aughing, screaming corpses daunt
O range pumpkins glowing bright
W ailing Reaper ready to fright
E normous old houses scare
E nter the mansion if you dare
N ightly happenings going on,
   In the morn they are all gone.

**Kieran Lockyer  (12)**
**Portchester School, Bournemouth**

# The World As I Know It

The world as I know it.
I feel like a misfit.
Everyone's so happy,
But I feel so crappy.
I don't like to talk about myself,
But this is how I feel.
Is this reality?
Because this feels so real.
I've had my cries,
I've told my lies.
People have gone now,
I miss them somehow.
I'm angry with them,
But I have to forgive them.
There's someone I love, but I can't say who,
Because I don't know, it could even be you.
It's getting better,
The weather's getting wetter.
It doesn't really fit,
It should rain when I'm sad, shouldn't it?
Maybe when it's all good,
I'll feel like I should.
But until then I'm sad, no one can help,
Only I can help myself, only I know who I am.
That didn't rhyme, but life's not a poem.
It doesn't all fit; you have to fix it to make it how you want it.
Fix yourself before you fix anyone else,
Then, when you're happy with yourself,
You can help others to be happy.

**Logan Partridge  (16)**
**Portchester School, Bournemouth**

# Fish In A Bowl

The fish was there
I tried not to stare
But it looked strange
I tried to grab it,
But it swam out of range.

It was an orange fish
As it moved in the water,
I heard a swish.
Out from behind a rock, came a second fish,
I though to myself, *mmm, this would make a nice dish.*

I dropped some food into the water
And out from another rock
Came the orange fish's daughter.
The orange fish began to splash its tail
Along with the other fish, it was determined not to fail
All of them wanted the food.

**Josh Kaye  (15)**
**Portchester School, Bournemouth**


# Frankenstein

F rankenstein, the green-headed monster
R aring to be born
A rgh! The thing's alive
N ever awoken before
K ind-hearted monster
E nding this way was never meant
N ot very happy
S tunned by the power
T he bolts on his neck are rusty with age
E verlasting
I t's the best moment of my life
N ever seen the light of day.

**Connor Clark  (12)**
**Portchester School, Bournemouth**

# Sport

Some love it, some hate it,
Some play it, some watch it,
Inside, outside,
Played all year round.

Children, adults, OAPs,
Sport is for everyone,
Even you and me.

Football, baseball, basketball,
All fun sports to play,
Played in the park, on a field,
Even on a walkway.

Competitions, tournaments, leagues and a cup,
Something that many people worship,
Cups and medals all part of the game,
Being the best is the aim.

Some love it, some hate it,
Some play it, some watch it,
Inside, outside,
Played all year round.

**Luke Bayliss  (15)**
**Portchester School, Bournemouth**


# Darkness

You're on your own,
No one, no friends, no family,
It's a world of darkness!
Your life depends on a man's best friend.
He can be your only family,
It depends on his guidance,
To get you through your life.
Don't get him wrong,
Or he won't learn about walking men,
Going out will teach him right,
This is the life of a blind man and his dog!

**Joe Jones  (15)**
**Portchester School, Bournemouth**

# Size 8 x 24

As I stand in the goal frame
Looking consciously at the football game,
Suddenly the attack make a charge
If I make a mistake I will get the blame.

Then from nowhere they shoot
Going on target since it left their boot,
Rolling across the ground coming towards me
So instead of catching it I block it with my foot.

I hoof the goal kick to a player
Who fumbles on the ball,
So I tell him to clear it as the call,
The striker tackles him and dribbles towards me
As the defender gets up from his fall.

So the player decides to shoot early in a dare
Just to try and put me in a scare,
The ball aims for the top corner, I start my jump
I save the ball and hit the ground with a bump.

As the game gets deeper
I realise I am the goalkeeper.

**Leo Abate  (15)**
**Portchester School, Bournemouth**


# It Seemed Like A Good Idea At The Time . . .

'It seemed like a good idea at the time,'
Is the spontaneous voice in everyone's mind,
A flux of power surges through our brain,
Causing the most controlled of us to go a bit insane.
For a few moments at least our plan is clear
Not hazed by drugs or fuelled by beer!
Our little impulses often go wrong
As do the explanations that follow on,
So I end on line number nine
Don't know why . . .
*Seemed like a good idea at the time!*

**Michael Nicholls  (15)**
**Portchester School, Bournemouth**

# Spiral Relationship

It's hard to adjust to a love like yours
When your emotions are swinging like two loose doors
I know that feelings can be hard to hide
When they're tearing and burning you up deep inside
Cos I know that there's nothing that I can do
When you stare at the stars with your face looking blue
But I know that I can't let you stare at the sky
When you're feeling down with a tear in your eye
For if I do let your sadness pass me by
When you're feeling different I will be the bad guy
And the bad guy's not the role I like to play
Not next week, not tomorrow, not today
So I'll say something sweet to make you forget
Whatever it is you so deeply regret
But what I love about us is that moment so strange
When all of our feelings are just out of range
And all that is left is just you and me
Anything else is just too hard to see
And I know now for sure that that moment is love
That beautiful thing more sweet than a dove
Because all I can do while lying still in my bed
Is stare at the ceiling with you in my head
And know that there's nowhere I'd rather be
Than shuffling along with you next to me.

**David Henon  (15)**
**Portchester School, Bournemouth**

## Survival

Make or break day has arrived,
Everyone thought it would get better by now,
But they were wrong,
The crowd are nervous, the manager silent,
Eleven men walk out; their fate is in their own hands,
The next ninety minutes will decide everything.

The atmosphere is tense,
Players grow angry with one another,
Nothing seems to be going the home team's way,
All eyes are on the clock as the ninety minute mark approaches,
Everyone goes silent; the last shot of the game has been struck,
The back of the net ripples, the ball settles on the ground silently,
The crowd erupts with cheer, their shouts can be heard everywhere
As the final whistle is sounded.

**Luke Tanswell  (15)**
**Portchester School, Bournemouth**


## What Is Life?

Life is love
Love is life
You can live without love
But what is life without love?

If I would die
I'd tell no lie
Just die hoping that you would be mine
You are love and love is life
If we had forever you'd be my wife.

**Donald Dowling  (15)**
**Portchester School, Bournemouth**

# Death

Death is everywhere
But is nowhere
It is imminent
Yet can't be predicted

Death is the end
But the beginning
Of a big adventure
That you cannot turn back on

That big adventure never stops
Yet we try to stop it
It is above us
It is what divides us
And in the dark, it strikes.

**Lloyd Harkcom (15)**
**Portchester School, Bournemouth**


# Crime

The police are surrounding,
The dogs are howling,
The robbers are prowling,
The drugs are mounting.

The kids are drinking,
The mothers are thinking,
The street lights are blinking,
What are you thinking?

Fight for the climb,
And not for the crime.
Don't step out of line,
Thanks for your time listening to my rhyme!

**James Ferrett (15)**
**Portchester School, Bournemouth**

## Thunder, Wind And Water

The cry of thunder is cruel to the ears
The crashing of the clouds, a war cry cheer
But a silver lining is yet to come
Not all is lost but not all is done.

The wind shapes the sea and the sky
It gives art to the waves and the clouds which go by
But anger the wind and you will see
The waves will grow and the sky will turn bleak.

The water is deep and goes on forever
The soothing blue is peaceful and calm
But become jealous of this deep blue friend
And you will soon see a bitter end.

**Daniel Payne (15)**
**Portchester School, Bournemouth**


## Food

Food is what we all need,
Not enough and you'll become a weed.

But people die every day,
From hunger and decay.

We should help all these people,
Because after all, we are all equal.

So next time you chuck food away,
Remember another person died today.

**Ben Heathman (15)**
**Portchester School, Bournemouth**

# The Ashes

Australia versus England are the teams,
The name 'the Ashes' is the theme.
They play for a tiny trophy known as the Urn,
It contains the ashes of some cricket bales that got the burn.
The biggest contest in the history of cricket,
Centre of attention, a twenty-two yard pitch known as the wicket.

For years on end the Aussies have been on top,
Up until this summer when they just went flop!
As the English nation came together in support,
The Aussie team were becoming distraught.
Many of the English watched it on TV,
But the most encouragement came from the stadium seats.

The Australians had some great stars on tour:
Clarke and Lee, but best of all, Shane Warne.
However, none compared to the English heroes that were born:
Flintoff, Harmison, Pietersen and Vaughan,
Those are just a pick of the best,
If I could, I'd name the rest!

Throughout the series there were many ups and downs,
Smiles and frowns.
But in the end, the nation rose in glee,
As they saw Michael Vaughan lift 'the Ashes' urn in victory!

**Kiran Patel  (15)**
**Portchester School, Bournemouth**


# Mouse

M ini in size
O utside in the cold all the time
U nafraid of the world around you
S tealing the food and comforts you need
E ating the farmer's precious grain.

**Samuel Cooke  (16)**
**Portchester School, Bournemouth**

# Under The Sea

I wonder what is down there in the ocean,
Maybe a load of fishy commotion,
They don't need any sun lotion.

Many species of shark,
But no underwater play park,
Must get dark.

And then all the fish,
Some go so fast, *swish*,
But some end up in a sushi dish.

Swimming around a pirate's treasure,
What do fish do in their time of leisure?
Being a fish isn't tremendous pleasure.

**Nick Woolner (15)**
**Portchester School, Bournemouth**


# Homeless

He has no life and no career,
He spends all day drinking beer.
He plays some tunes to raise some cash,
So off his dealer he can get some hash.
But now he sees that his life is bad,
Taking hash every day just makes him mad.
He gets some new clothes and sets to find a job,
Only to be mugged by an angry yob.
Now he is back to sleeping rough,
Being homeless is pretty tough.

**David Love (15)**
**Portchester School, Bournemouth**

# Mr Moor

Mr Moor, Mr Moor
Creeping down the corridor
*Eh, eh, eheh, eh.*
Mr Moor has very sharp teeth
Mr Moor does not like quiche
*Eh, eh, eheh, eh.*
Mr Moor, Mr Moor, Mr Moor
*Eh, eh, eheh, eh.*
Mr Moor has pointy fingers
Mr Moor doesn't like fish fingers
*Eh, eh, eheh, eh.*
Mr Moor, Mr Moor
Creeping down the corridor
*Eh, eh, eheh, eh*
Mr Moor has very big feet
Mr Moor doesn't like treats
Mr Moor, Mr Moor
Creeping down the corridor.

**Billy Player  (13)**
**Portchester School, Bournemouth**


# The Desert

The desert is a quiet place
There is a lot of space
There is hardly anyone there
It is so hot you have to be bare
The desert feels like it goes on forever
Walk in the desert if you dare!

**James Plunkett  (11)**
**Portchester School, Bournemouth**

# Late For Dinner

I opened my front door
I was really unsure
I was late for dinner
Today I was not his winner.
When I came in
What a sin
He threw his beer glass at me
'Don't do that Daddy.'
I shouted for Mum
'Shut up you scum'
Dad got his belt
So I knelt.
He whipped me hard
He said I was a piece of lard
There I lay sprawled across the floor
I am not his little boy anymore.
He said he would stop calling me thick head
But four days later I was dead.

**David Pettet  (11)**
**Portchester School, Bournemouth**


# The Giraffe

A neck the size of a lamp post
Brown chickenpox all over
As gigantic as a two-storey building
And eats a ton of clover.

It lives in a huge zoo
And it takes a lot of staff
To look after this big animal
It's the mighty old giraffe!

While everybody looks at him
He stands around all day
But to see him at the zoo
You need to go and pay!

**James Cooper  (11)**
**Portchester School, Bournemouth**

# World: Blessing Or Curse?

I stand in legions with others to gaze upon this wretched
world crumbling,
Watching it slip through my fingers into a darkening spell of
despair and grief,
Myself and company seek to rid this world of its worn and
faded robes,
To rid it of all its immoral reasoning,
To bring it forthwith into its own unique path of hope,
To see it fight back, to win.
All seems placid for the lost people of this Earth,
No hope for them, no valour,
This is true,
They see the world with no passion, no inspiration, no kindness,
Just to sit there in their fake happiness,
And so they stare, stare into nothingness,
To hopefully escape the reality, the truth.
And so I stand, hopefully not alone, to fend away this wicked truth,
To hopefully see it quiver and flee,
But one day it will catch up and bind us into old age.
It will close around as if it was a poisonous smog,
A cage for us to be never set free,
Standing alone in the dark,
Waiting, hoping for someone, someone to see.

**Kit Moulding  (15)**
**Portchester School, Bournemouth**


# It!

It is a word that has no meaning,
It is weird and even deceiving,
It is a word which gives out feeling,
It stands out as if it was gleaming.

It's so far away, it seems like I'm dreaming,
Lost in a cloud it shines out, beaming,
This is the end, it still has no meaning,
It is still weird and still deceiving.

**George Lawrence  (15)**
**Portchester School, Bournemouth**

# Help Me!

On Monday you hid my bag,
On Tuesday you took my chair,
On Wednesday you stole my pen,
On Thursday you broke my pencil,
On Friday you pulled my hair,
On Saturday I met with my friends,
On Sunday I played with my nan,
On Monday you hid my bag,
On Tuesday you took my chair,
On Wednesday you stole my pen,
On Thursday you pulled my hair,
On Friday - I wasn't there . . .

**Matthew Watkins  (11)**
**Portchester School, Bournemouth**


# The Parrot

I'm happy and loud in the day
But quiet at night.
My beautiful wings so sweet and sound
Blues, reds and white mix into the night.
Most people love me,
Some people hate me.
I mimic them, tease them
And they cage me.
But all in all I'm more beautiful than anything
And they will never make me as boring as a pigeon!

**Matthew Sacchi  (11)**
**Portchester School, Bournemouth**

# Crooks

*(Based on 'Of Mice And Men' by John Steinbeck)*

I'm all alone,
Isn't everyone?
I'm bullied every day,
Isn't everyone?
My books are my only friends,
The others taunt me 'cause I'm black,
Thanks to a horse I've got a crooked back
And not got amazing looks,
Is that why my name is Crooks?

I tend the horses,
All alone,
My only visitors are the boss and Slim,
Neither are my friends,
At least they talk to me,
A guy needs someone to talk to you know.
I guess things might change,
Before my dream ends.

**Matthew Allen (15)**
**Portchester School, Bournemouth**

# Poetry

P oems are literature's finest work
O ur one escape into a different world
E asy to read
T errible to write
R hyming is what we try
Y ielding our imaginations, goodbye.

**Ewan Leckie (15)**
**Portchester School, Bournemouth**

# I'm Forever Blowing Bubbles

Turning up to watch the match
ICF they'll want to smash
The hell out of the other team
But that's not what we're here to see
This could go down in history.

Thousands of people in their seats
As the chant begins they rise to their feet
'I'm forever blowing bubbles, pretty bubbles in the air'
The opposition are shocked and can't help but stare.

Dreams and hopes echo through the stands
People shouting, smiling and clapping their hands
As the Hammers make an entrance for the fans to see
The north and south stands erupt with glee
This was what we're here to see
This *will* go down in history.

**James Lofts (16)**
**Portchester School, Bournemouth**

# Fish

One day there was a fish called Sam
Who met a girl fish called Pam
They swam around the pool
Until Pam swam into a wall
Sad Sam was so lonely now
He really missed his favourite pal
He ate a lot of spicy ham
Until one day he went *bam!*

**Christian Ridout (12)**
**Portchester School, Bournemouth**

# Volcano

'It's going to erupt, it's going to erupt,'
The heat started to make my clothes crease,
At this time it was all corrupt,
The volcano was hot but had not released.

'Argh! Run, it's bubbling, it's bubbling,'
It had got so hot I stripped from my fleece,
The volcano rocks were now crumbling,
The volcano was hot but had not released.

'Quick, quick, save yourself, just run,'
It was now flowing down the streets, people had to flee,
The only way to run was across the River McGhee,
The volcano was so hot it was anything but fun.

People were running as if there was a killing spree,
We didn't know how, we didn't know why it was erupting right now,
You had to run as fast as you could to get free,
The volcano was so hot it was anything but fun.

I'm so sorry, I'm so sorry you couldn't get out in time,
It took my dad, it took my brother and also took my mother,
The village was ruined, crushed,
The volcano was fast, it was steaming and the injured
                                    were screaming.

Why, why, why, did my family have to die?
Under the burning rubble I heard a cry,
I tried to help the injured as they had a chance,
The volcano was fast, it was steaming, and the injured
                                    were screaming.

**Ashley Calderwood  (12)**
**Portchester School, Bournemouth**

# The Hillsborough Disaster

On the 15th of April in the year '89,
I lost many fellow supporters o' mine.
We were having a laugh when he heard the first cry,
At the tragic disaster in the Leppings Lane end.

Between the supporters panic broke out,
We were all full o' doubt.
Most of the people who died were all the same age as scouts,
At the tragic disaster in the Leppings Lane end.

The emergency services drive,
Supporters tried to survive.
Overall, ninety-six Liverpudlians lost their lives,
At the tragic disaster in the Leppings Lane end.

**Sam Le Feaux  (12)**
**Portchester School, Bournemouth**


# Friends

Sometimes these people can drive you mad.
Sometimes these people can get you in trouble.
Sometimes these people can even get you hurt.
But these are the people we trust with our feelings.
These are the people whose company we enjoy.
These are the people who could hurt us most.
But they don't.
Because a friend is special.
A friend sticks with you till the very end.
For this is what it takes to be a good friend.

**Haydon Palmer  (16)**
**Portchester School, Bournemouth**

# Girls

They can be good,
They can be bad,
They make you happy,
They make you sad,
Some are evil,
Some are nice,
They'll cheat once,
And they'll cheat twice,
They'll make you smile,
They'll make you cry,
In the end,
They'll say bye-bye,
You won't let them go,
Without a fight,
So who actually knows,
What a real girl is like?

**Kristyen Denham  (16)**
**Portchester School, Bournemouth**


# Poppy

This is for my pussycat, Poppy,
Who was very jumpy and hoppy,
She was hit by a car,
But she went so far . . .

The 13th - unlucky for some,
I never used to believe it!
But honestly, now I do!
Because she was killed on the 13th September.

Miss you, Pops.

**Katie Beckingham  (14)**
**Regents Park Community College, Southampton**

# Shooting Star

Shadows danced around my room,
As light started to dim,
Darkness would be coming soon,
Letting nightmares in.

Out of the window,
Something caught my eye,
A subtle glow under the moonlight
A shooting star passing by.

It floated down from above,
So I grabbed it tight,
We soared up like a dove
And flew into the night.

In the inky-black space,
We passed millions of stars,
Watching aliens race,
In their hovering cars.

Flying back to my room,
I saw it in sight,
I passed the man in the moon
As he waved me goodnight.

Snuggled in my blanket,
My eyes began to close,
On my face a smile set,
My secret no one knows.

**Rachael Murray  (13)**
**Regents Park Community College, Southampton**

# Autumn

This is the time of year when,
Everyone walks across a red and gold carpet,
That seems to be everywhere,
Leading anywhere.
This is the time of year when,
The birds start to think of the cold months ahead
And begin to flock to the warmer countries.
This is the time of year when,
The squirrels are rapidly searching for nuts
And storing them,
Where they can be kept for food during hibernation.
This is the time of year when,
Everybody starts wearing woolly jumpers
And fireworks fill the sky,
With blues and emerald greens
And the frost rolls in.

This is the time of year called . . .
Autumn!

**Jemma Gilbert (13)**
**Regents Park Community College, Southampton**


# Poem

The teachers stand, dark and tall,
Their eyes narrow, icy and cruel,
No feelings left in their bones,
Their classrooms now their homes.
The class that was once dead and sad,
Has now left school,
Thank God for that.
The dungeon cells they were kept in,
What did they do that was such a sin?
And once the class is gone and dead,
The teachers will move on,
To kill the rest.

**Carmen Jones (13)**
**Regents Park Community College, Southampton**

# Changing World

I walk down the crowded streets,
Looking at what our world has become.
Tiny children, barely clothed, begging on street corners,
Tears trickling down their grubby faces.
A homeless man wrapped in an old blanket,
Like a discarded piece of rubbish,
Snuggled up to his sad looking dog.
People staring in disgust as they pass,
He doesn't care, he's used to it.
Graffiti-covered parks, walls, benches and more.
However, is it the world that is changing,
Or is it the people who walk past without a care?
They're happy, so what does it matter?

So is it the world that has changed?
*No!*
The people have changed the world.

**Jade Mintrim  (13)**
**Regents Park Community College, Southampton**


# Silver Eye

Silver eye gazing down at the Earth,
A lonely giant that controls the seas.
Harvest, oak, blue and storm,
These are just four of the twelve that we see.
We might see it one night, may not the next,
It illuminates the sky with the help of the stars.
The moon is a goddess, beautiful and calm,
Her friends are Orion, Venus and Mars.

**Laura Morrell  (13)**
**Regents Park Community College, Southampton**

# Rose

A flower from a garden,
A rose of ruby-red,
Taken by a young child,
After the many tears she shed.
'Flower, flower, from the ground,
You'll stay with me for life,'
Then she wiped away her salty tears
And forgot about her strife.
She trudged on to her heartless house
And listened at the door,
The house seemed calm and empty
And the shouting was no more.
A small smile crept across her face
As she entered the peaceful house,
She was surprised to see her father sitting
As quiet as a mouse.
'Your mother said she loves you
And will contact you some day,
It's me she couldn't live with . . .'
And he dabbed a tear away.
The girl will never forget that day,
When she waited by the phone,
Clutching onto her ruby rose,
Feeling so alone.
Days and weeks and months passed,
She's still waiting for that call,
With the flower wilting in her hands,
She watched the final petal fall.

**Beth Cooke  (13)**
**Regents Park Community College, Southampton**

# A Mistake!

I clench his hand,
As his name is called,
It's his turn now,
His body so mauled!

I walk in the room,
He's followed along,
It looks dull and dreary,
With a scent so strong!

He trembles with fear,
His hands start to shake,
It is time I could leave,
Maybe a mistake!

Hours and hours,
As I wait and wait,
People go in
And come out a fit state!

Finally he comes,
Still with wounds and cuts,
Thanks to drink driving,
His life now in guts!

I'll just have a couple,
That's what everyone thinks,
It could cost a life,
Just a hit in a blink!

**Katrina Loizou  (13)**
**Regents Park Community College, Southampton**

# Winter

Mint-green grass crunching crisply under your freezing feet
Your breath hangs undisturbed in the air
The unclothed trees huddle and groan in the bitter breeze
The last squirrel scampers quickly into its cosy hiding place
                                        for the coming months
A warm, inviting glow radiates from the frosted windows
The blazing fire dances merrily behind the grate
The vivid hats and gloves assemble comfortably, warming on
                                        the radiator
The little children gaze patiently out the window
A single snowflake drifts gently to the ground.

**Eloise Lavington  (13)**
**Regents Park Community College, Southampton**


# Summer

The sky is blue,
The sun is gold,
The butterflies flutter,
Beautiful and bold.

The adults laugh,
The children play,
'Can't wait until the summer again,'
Soon everyone will say.

**Ella Dixon  (13)**
**Regents Park Community College, Southampton**

# Disasters

Hurricanes, tornadoes, tsunamis and storms,
Crashes and flashes, flooding and flame,
Damage, destruction, misery and fear,
These are events that can happen at any time of year.
Katrina and Stanley, Rita and more,
All recent events that affect mainly the poor,
Now homeless, bereaved, no possessions or home,
These disasters tell of our future to come.
Nature is kind but can also be cruel,
To landscapes and people there is no strict rule.
The answer lies in a united world,
Where everyone helps those in need, wherever they are,
We must all join together to help fellow man,
To minimise the misery whenever we can.

**Libby Thornton  (13)**
**Regents Park Community College, Southampton**


# The Storm

The storm flashes lightning, the midnight sky,
The storm flashes as the clouds go by.
The lightning flashes through the air,
One unforgettable, haunting nightmare.
A happy, blue sky is covered in a sack,
The happy, blue sky is turned to black.
Finally, the sun comes out
And the flowers can now sprout.

**Maryam Anibaba  (13)**
**Regents Park Community College, Southampton**

# Pop Idol

Walking down the crowded aisles,
Looking at the grins and smiles.

Winners here and losers there,
People check their clothes and hair.

Sitting still, butterflies now,
Thinking about Simon Cowell.

Will I win or will I lose?
Only three judges that can choose.

Here I go, time to sing,
Oh my God, I've got in!

Running out, shouting loud,
My family will be really proud.

All my thanks to Simon Cowell!

**Danielle Meakin  (15)**
**Ryeish Green School, Reading**


# Judging

Singin' a song down the mike,
Sounds terrible, take a hike.
Next contestant comin' on,
How'd he get through, was it a con?
Onto a cute guy, let's hear him sing,
He can't sing a single thing.
A nice little plain girl, not really good lookin',
Hearin' her voice, wow she is cookin'!
That's it, you're going through,
Another guy, wow he's through too!
The end of the line, audition's at an end,
My head hurts, drivin' me round the bend.
There's talent and strops, there's tears and laughter,
As everyone lives happily ever after.

**Hannah Crozier  (15)**
**Ryeish Green School, Reading**

# The Destroyers Of Hopes And Dreams

I step into the room,
Eyeing the judges with pride,
Although I feel failure loom,
All I want to do is hide.

I introduce myself with a smile,
The judges give me confirmation to go,
I get stage fright for a while,
But then I start singing and let it flow.

I sing with my heart,
I sing with my mind,
But the eyes of the judges dart
And I wonder if they'll be kind.

I finish the song with strength in my voice,
I see the judges' eyes,
And leave a moment to rejoice,
I'm going to do this and win the prize.

I get nods of stardom and fame,
Knowing I've passed this round,
But will things ever be the same,
With my voice and its sound?

**Natasha Turner (14)**
**Ryeish Green School, Reading**


# No!

I step out onto the stage, the light on me,
I look backstage and they shout, 'Start performing.'
The crowd starts to cheer as I open my mouth,
I'm sweating as much as I did in the south.
Then I fall back to Earth with a big, massive *thud!*
I think to myself, *my gosh, my God, crud!*
Nicky stands up and says, 'Hello . . .'
Then Simon shouts a big, massive *'No!'*

**Victoria Aldridge (15)**
**Ryeish Green School, Reading**

# Pop Idol

Streams of blazing, coloured lights,
Rejection, tears, full of frights,
People singing, laughter heard,
Backstage passes, stardom stirred.

Filming, production, abusive remarks,
Camera, action, performing arts,
The crowds, the fans, Saturday nights,
Futures held, within sight.

Walking towards the doors held still,
Open fate, chance and will,
My heart a-thumping in my chest,
I need to sit, I need to rest.

Cold sweat dripping down my face,
I want to win, it's like a race,
Simon Cowell, an evil tease,
Singing loud, trembling knees.

I've made it through, I've got the chance,
Success draws near, held in a trance,
I run, I run, I do not stop,
I reach my mum, I fall, I drop.

**Laura Russell (15)**
**Ryeish Green School, Reading**


# No Room For The Hesitant

Main stage drama and tears mixed in,
That's what Pop Idol's about, abandoning your kin.
For what? Stardom and fame?
What's going to last out of this horrible game?

Treacherous scheming, arriving with their game plans,
Some use sympathy, some who can't say they can.
But when the time comes and they choke,
Who's going to be there? This new-found fame or your regular bloke?

**Juhi Saini (15)**
**Ryeish Green School, Reading**

# Water Skiing

Anxious bodies, shaking hands
Standing on the rocky lands
A boat draws near, the fear strikes
'Get in the water! Hold the rope!'

Grip gets tighter, water parts.
Skis kick in, the lift goes up.
Eyes held shut with fear.

Weak at the knees, pull at the rope,
Down you go, but trust in the boat
And up you go, elegant and slow.

I feel the breeze in my hair,
The speed beneath my arms
I did it! I'm up!
The water's in my toes.

**Daisy Skepelhorn (12)**
**St Antony's Leweston School, Sherborne**


# My Future With My Connemaras

In the future I can see
Some ponies grazing beside me
One is dun, one is bay
And the other one is dappled grey

Remus is the handsome dun
Whizzy the pretty bay one
Lady is the dappled grey
A champion pony in her day

All these ponies are there for me
To compete on successfully
Working Hunter at the Horse of the Year
Or Best of Breed at Olympia.

This is the future I foresee
On these beautiful Connemaras bred for me.

**Charlotte Walters (11)**
**St Antony's Leweston School, Sherborne**

# The Old, Pink Pig

My family and I once had a pink pig
He was hugely fat and hugely big
He slept and ate all day long
Wrapped up in hay whilst singing a song

The old pig did this every day
He would not stop any which way
So at last we all then said, 'This has to end'
But it didn't happen to our little pink friend

'Cause we tried giving him less food
But then he went into a mood
We honestly tried to make him stop
But he got into more of a strop

We then eventually gave up
And sat down and had a cup
Of hot chocolate, coffee and tea
Whilst watching Desperate Housewives on TV

Whilst everyone was indoors
Outside the rain did pour
And when this happened there was a surprise
Outside in the sty the pig changed size

When my mother saw this she went insane
Because the pig had grown a mane
When my father got up and had a yawn
He saw the pig had grown some horns

He grew some wings and then turned blue
He looked at us and then he flew
The whole town could see him, he flew so high
He flew to a cloud up in the sky

The pig then left us and went away
To join a circus the very next day
The pig now lives in Hollywood with his lady friend, Kylie
And once a month he visits us and we all go to the sea.

**Hattie Field (11)**
**St Antony's Leweston School, Sherborne**

# Winter

She flows through the towns and cities,
Leaving a trail of frost behind her.
She sweeps her long cloak over the dark blue skies,
Mist falling and gently suspended above the ground.

Her blue lips mutter something,
Sending a chill to the earth around her
And where her graceful feet step,
The soil beneath turns to ice.

Winter's white-blue hair flows freely
In the howling wind,
Her sapphire eyes gleam
As snowflakes quietly tumble to the floor.

She leaps from tree to tree
In the mysterious wood,
Skipping gracefully through the dripping rain,
The snow getting deeper.

In a clearing in the wood, Winter sees a small lake,
She slowly bends down and puts her fingertips slowly
In the fresh, cool, sparkling water.
As she takes them out, the shimmering pool freezes over.

As Winter drifts out of the wood, she sees the sky,
It is pink and the dawning sun has just risen.
She knows her work is done,
Winter hovers off, ready to return next year.

**Hennie Helliwell (11)**
**St Antony's Leweston School, Sherborne**

# From The Eyes Of A Deep-Sea Diver

The deep-sea diver is now submerged
In a mysterious underwater planet.
At first, he is entwined in slimy seaweed and murky water.
He carries on descending, starting off slowly,
But all the time getting faster and faster.
Swirling and tumbling down and down.
But then his vision clears and he is able to see again.
The water is beginning to become clear.
The diver can now see all different hues of coloured coral,
Oysters with stunning pearls inside, lying motionless
on the sandy seabed.
Exotic fish are swimming around
And hiding behind rocks from their intruder.
A lone stingray darts across his vision,
Gliding and dancing like a ship in full sail.
The diver swims in an eastward direction
Towards a dark, misshapen silhouette.
A ship that has not seen the world above
for at least one hundred years,
Lies dormant on the seabed,
Waiting to be awoken from its slumber by the deep-sea diver.
Perhaps its hidden secrets should never be revealed!

**Taliska Baden  (11)**
St Antony's Leweston School, Sherborne


# The Shipwreck

Up on the rocks perched the Lady Jane Grey,
So seemingly complete yet full of dismay,
Only yesterday playing cat and mouse with the waves,
But now just a memory in a blurred haze,
Despite the frame of the solid oak wood,
The storm was able to do the worst it could,
The mast still dreaming about the dances in the sky,
But now the only thing to do, is cry.

**Chloë Henderson  (13)**
St Antony's Leweston School, Sherborne

# Sweeties Through The Years

My mummy sometimes tells me how sweeties used to be,
With pear drops, lollipops and Jelly Tots for only a halfpenny.

My grandparents' days were different too, my mummy often says,
They only got given sweeties on very special days.

And then there are my sisters, who drive me up the wall,
With stories of how Curly Wurlys never used to be that small.

But then of course Mum tells me how bad they are for me,
These Haribos will rot my teeth and put me off my tea.

If I'm truly honest, I don't really care,
If, when I reach eighty-seven, I find my mouth is bare!

I'll get some teeth from the dentist and eat soup instead
And take them out at night-time and leave them by my bed.

**Jade Letts**
**St Antony's Leweston School, Sherborne**


# Friends

A friend is a person that is always with you
In bad and good times
Is like a brother, like a part of your family
That always helps you.

He doesn't care if you are near or far
He is always thinking of you and never forgets you
He always remembers your birthday
And he is the first one to congratulate you.

A friend never leaves you alone
And always tries to make you happy
Even if he gets mad, he tries to stop the fight
Because he never wants to lose your friendship.
If you are far of a friend, never forget him
And that's why friends are the best.

**Monica Sanchez (13)**
**St Antony's Leweston School, Sherborne**

# My Sad Horse

He's a planet,
The king of the sea,
Neptune is he.

My sad horse,
Stands in his stable,
Looking out for me.
He looks around for me,
His little head looks over the door.

We trot him up and down the yard,
But still lame is he.
We take him to the vet,
The vet says, 'Put him out in the field.'

We do as he says.
I open the gate wide,
I let go of Neptune,
He does a giant buck,
He tears off down the field bucking wildly.
His friends come rearing,
Glitz and Bramble,
They go galloping by his side,
Down the field.
I love him, he's the best, that's he!

**Florence Pisani  (11)**
**St Antony's Leweston School, Sherborne**

# Give In

I once smiled at the sun
And it warmed me,
I once winked at the moon
And it charmed me,
I once whispered to the stars
And they inspired me,
Now I wail to the wind
And it chills me,
Now I scream to the night
And it fills me with despair,
For it shows no one cares,
This chase you win,
I give in,
Those spangled beams now entangle me,
You caught me,
Give in, for the world has no compassion.

**Isabelle Barber  (12)**
**St Antony's Leweston School, Sherborne**


# Girl

I am a girl
But I am no ordinary girl
I am not a girl whose best friend is a diamond
I'm more like a man whose best friend is a dog.

I go on adventures
Into the wild
Looking for wild boars
And reindeer.

Next I am a spy
Watching my brother like a hawk
I don't want to be a pretty little girl
Who's locked up inside a house
I want to go and explore
I'm no ordinary girl.

**Rowan Skellern  (11)**
**St Antony's Leweston School, Sherborne**

# The Future

The future will be bright, brighter than now.
It will have flying pigs and flying cars.

The future will be clean, cleaner than now.
There will be magic in the air.

Wizards, witches, flying all around.
There will be no horror and no death
And there will be no illness ever again.

People will discover more and more planets
And perhaps might even land on a new planet
That has not been found yet.

They will invent more and more medication
And stop wasting things like oil and food
And stop chucking things into the sea.

Make people stop killing animals like elephants
And stop killing whales,
Then God will look down on us like He is now
And will make the future a happier place to live.

**Chloé Taylor  (11)**
**St Antony's Leweston School, Sherborne**


# The Tiger

Your eyes aflame,
Your nose a-twitching,
As you lie in the green, green grass.

Your mouth wide open,
Your tongue half out,
As you study your hopeful prey.

Your feet poised,
As you go for the pounce
And your claws dig in.

What a wonderful creature a tiger is,
As it lies in the green, green grass.

**Daisy Crichton  (12)**
**St Antony's Leweston School, Sherborne**

# Future

There are 34 aliens,
200 slugs
And everyone has four toes.
Our leader is a two-headed freak!
People wonder,
If we are in a dream,
While they drink a mug of hot chocolate with some cream.

The sky is red,
The grass is orange,
The trees are purple with roots on the top!
The birds are on the ground
And people are flying
And dogs take them for walks!

So I think you'll agree with me
That the future is *freaky!*

**Rachel Hill  (11)**
**St Antony's Leweston School, Sherborne**


# Dearest

Round as a ball
Sometimes became roses' thorns
Stayed with me
Held me warmly when I was sad
Carried me on a back when I was hurt
Bounced with me when I was happy
I felt pain on my red cheek when I did wrong
Lots of affection
I resisted again and again
'I can do anything about myself,' I said
Keeping eyes as a mild moon opened in the dark sky
Stand by my side
If I can flap as a bird, I will fly to your side . . .

**Hanayo Uchida  (14)**
**St Antony's Leweston School, Sherborne**

# Alone Is A Lonely Word

Tell me why you left me
All alone in such an awful world?
Tell me why you didn't see
How much your leaving would hurt me?
And now I cry every day
And now I feel there's nothing to say,
Because you, my only reason to live, is gone.
Tell me where the light is that once shone upon my life?
Before, I could handle anything, any strife,
Now I just give up hope,
Now I find it hard to cope,
Because every time I think of you,
I think of all the things that we could do,
If you were still here
And I still feel as though you may reappear
But you don't.
Please tell me why you won't?
Because life is nothing without you,
Life is nothing without you here too,
But the thing that hurts me most,
Is if you were here because you felt you were supposed to be here,
That is my worst fear.
What if you do not miss me?
What if I am to bend upon my knee
And say a prayer that you will come . . .?
Even though this may seem mad to some,
When that is not what you would want,
That is the thought that will forever taunt . . .
Me!

**Violet Thompson  (13)**
**St Antony's Leweston School, Sherborne**

# Dreams, Dreams, Glorious Dreams

Some evenings I sit and dream
And think about what fun it would have been.
To be a pencil, sitting in a pencil case
What fun it would have been.

Some evenings I sit and think
About what it would be like to be a kitchen sink.
Washing, scrubbing, sitting, bubbling
Yes, it would be fun to be a kitchen sink.

Some evenings I sit and wonder and really just ponder
About what it would be like
To be a brilliant child celebrity
Singing here, singing there, singing almost everywhere.

And then I thought, *Now I see!*
*Now I see what I want to be!*
*I don't want to be a kitchen sink*
*Made of copper, steel or zinc!*
*Nor a rubber, ruler or pencil*
*Not any kind of utensil!*

No, what I really want to be
Is not him, her you or thee.
But what I really want to be
Is just plain, little, old me!

**Kitty Whittell (11)**
**St Antony's Leweston School, Sherborne**

# Birthday

At my first birthday
I had chocolate cake
A great big party
And lots of presents

At my third birthday
I had strawberry cake
This time I had no party
I was at Disneyland
Having buckets of fun!

When I was five
I had a piñata
Which I broke with my friends
And ate all the candy I got!

When I was six
I got sick
And had medicine
But also a Twix

Finally, I'm ten
I will have carrot cake
My favourite one, I should say
I will have a pyjama party
And sleep with all my friends
Talking till 5 o'clock
When we'll go to bed!

**Sofia Vidal  (13)**
**St Antony's Leweston School, Sherborne**

# She

She stops and stares,
And wonders, what
This young man's face
Reminds her of.
His strange dark eyes,
His thick black hair,
The way he flinches at her glare.
He shuffles uneasily
And hesitates to speak,
The silence is awkward,
Her knees become weak.
He's guilty, she knows it,
He grins and turns,
She opens her mouth,
But the words she must learn.
A shock on her arm,
Her mother's close face,
Only to find,
That she is awake.

**Annabel Staib  (13)**
**St Antony's Leweston School, Sherborne**


# Rain

Rain, rain everywhere,
On my jumper,
In my hair,
When the rain splashes down,
My mummy always gives a frown,
Water gushing down the street,
Where all the children like to meet,
When the sun comes out to play,
I always say, *hip, hip, hooray!*

**Sophie Saunders  (11)**
**St Antony's Leweston School, Sherborne**

# What Shall I Be?

What do I want to be?
A tree, a bee?
No, deep down,
What do I want to be?

I thought I'd like to be a poet
And not know it.
But as you can see,
I'm worse at that than climbing trees!

Then I thought, I could be bad . . .
Are you kidding?
I'd be totally sad!

Then I thought I could be the best,
Better than all the rest,
But I don't want to become obsessed!
I still don't know what I want to be . . .

Oh, why didn't I stick
To just being me?

**Louise Newton  (13)**
**St Antony's Leweston School, Sherborne**


# No-Man's-Land

There was a line,
A line that no one could see.
There was a line,
A line that split a country.
There was a line,
Where armies gave up lives.
There was a line,
Where many good people died.
There was a line,
Where generals feared to stand.
There was a line,
In 1914 called no-man's-land.

**Alex Beer  (13)**
**St Antony's Leweston School, Sherborne**

# Mist

Mist danced silently,
Her pearly robes flowing behind her.
Moon smiled as she saw her child.

Mist danced through a village,
Leaving a trail of white darkness
Like a snail's silver track.

Mist danced alone,
To a song without words,
By a composer who never existed.

Her dance led her to a forest,
Where she paused,
Out of breath.

Then Mist danced
Into the clouds
From where she had come.

**Bettina Rogerson (11)**
**St Antony's Leweston School, Sherborne**


# Autumn Creeps In

The leaves have fallen from the trees
And cascade to the floor making a golden carpet
Squirrels scamper about
Collecting food for their winter pantries
Bushes are bejewelled with crimson berries
The ground sparkles with frost
The colourful flowers of summer close up
The sun becomes low in the sky
And the night becomes longer
Fields are golden with stubble
And the mist is low on the ground
And everything turns golden-brown
As autumn creeps in.

**Georgie Hagenbuch (13)**
**St Antony's Leweston School, Sherborne**

# Stair Thumper

*(This is dedicated to my mum and dad)*

I miss you thumping upstairs at night
And you always made sure that I was asleep.
But I would be on my side, facing the wall,
So you thought I was asleep, but then you turned away.

You would answer my every need.
I would do mean things, but you were always there.
I planned to run away,
But you changed that.

At one stage, I would talk,
You worried and cared for me,
It went on for a bit, but you talked and understood,
You said you loved me just as much, in fact more.

Then one night I made a worrying noise,
You thought I was the TV then you called the ambulance.
Then I was sick all over you, when we arrived at the hospital
And you brought my favourite ted.

I miss you thumping up the stairs at night.

**Emma Trollope-Bellew (12)**
**St Antony's Leweston School, Sherborne**


# Future

In the future I will see
Spaceships flying over me,
Blue jumpsuits will be worn
All rules will be torn,
All land will be ice
All food will be nice,
We will live in houses of gold
We will be very old,
All animals will be extinct
All humans will always stink,
Animals will die that's for sure
Time will always be gone.

**India Boon (11)**
**St Antony's Leweston School, Sherborne**

# The Story Of Flames

Flames are sometimes one of the most silent creatures
But can also crackle like the Devil
Like a horse galloping through the night
It is like dancers dancing a beautiful unfinished song
Or a knife blade melting under sweltering heat
You could say it's like a sad tale never undone
Perhaps the finest of spices
It's an unspoken picture taken in one shot
A firebird shedding one last tear
Maybe a deadly mushroom singing its final song
Biting into a lemon for the first time
Vultures rotating around, screaming in the despair of their life
A suffering child pleading, 'No more!'
It can catch your eye with the smallest flicker of light
A howling dog limping through the deserted wind
A sensation like never before
Hypnotic glare staring at you forever
Until it burns into ashes and blows away
Into the darkness forever and ever.

**Marianna Warley  (11)**
**St Antony's Leweston School, Sherborne**


# The Rainy Day

*Drip, drop, drip, drop,*
Went the rain outside her bedroom window
She planned to go out to the town and the shops
Now she'd have to stay home and sew.

*Drip, drop, drip, drop,*
It was sun she'd asked for, not soggy, wet rain,
It ruined her plans,
Oh, what a shame!

*Crash!* Went the thunder,
*Bang!* Went the lightning,
Oh, how she wondered,
When the *drip, drop* would stop.

**Francesca Damant  (13)**
**St Antony's Leweston School, Sherborne**

# My Poem

Far, far away
In the land of Nod
A fairy flew
And a dwarf did plod.

Far, far away
In the land of Nod
Where people have wings
And magic bells ring.

Far, far away
In the land of Nod
Where dinosaurs roam
And the sea does foam.

Far, far away
In the land of Nod
A boy does sleep!

**Jennifer Kerslake  (13)**
**St Antony's Leweston School, Sherborne**


# Autumn

Autumn leaves are falling down
Twirling, twisting, falling
Making a carpet of golden leaves
On the soft green ground

Glossy conkers fall and crack
Squirrels busy scurrying and scuttling
Storing away the fruits of the trees
For their winter's rest

Animals shy, hiding from the cold
Away from the sharp of the frost and snow
Sleeping, dreaming, keeping warm
Getting ready for the new spring.

**Lucy Gregory  (12)**
**St Antony's Leweston School, Sherborne**

*Young Writers - POP! Southern England*

# What Will The Future Be Like?

What will we eat?
Maybe we will eat pills
Or maybe just fruit and veg
No one knows.

How will we travel?
Maybe through the stars
Or perhaps by spaceship
No one knows.

Will people still go to school
Or will we learn by computers?
Will the teachers be robotic?
No one knows.

Does anyone know what happens in the future?
No one knows
But it looks like an exciting future
And I do know that what I've just written, is history!

**Grace James (13)**
**St Antony's Leweston School, Sherborne**

# The Future

The future is today
And tomorrow
There is no looking back
Anticipation, hope, expectation
Dread, or nervousness
Sick in my stomach
Feels like a bad car journey
Or too much fried food!
Fearless or frightened
We can only hope
That for us
In our world
We have a future.

**Anna Knipe (13)**
**St Antony's Leweston School, Sherborne**

# Autumn Leaves

A lone leaf flutters down,
Across the autumnal sky.
Followed by many others
Constantly floating by.

They land on the ground
Forming mounds of brown and gold.
Stopping the summer grass
Becoming very wet and cold.

A hedgehog snuffles through the leaves
Looking for a place to hide
He finds his home amongst the mounds
Which have dropped and died.

These are my thoughts on autumn
Of which I have seen ten.
The leaves are beginning to fall now
As the season comes again.

**April Kosky  (11)**
**St Antony's Leweston School, Sherborne**


# The Future Is Yours!

Destroyers and saviours their plans were drawn,
The Earth in the middle, ravaged and torn.
Derelict cities under dark skies
Only light from the clouds floating by,
The only living things are the flowers and trees
And some single-celled life that floats in the seas.
This is the story of your future and past,
Every breath you take is closer to your last.
Make your life count is the gist of the story,
Let your children live a life of glory.
Value all that's living, treat it with respect,
Stop all this wasting, ruin and neglect.
This is your chance to mend your ways,
Don't make your life the end of days.

**Sophie Danby  (12)**
**St Antony's Leweston School, Sherborne**

# Ice Cream Thief

The perfect place up in the sky,
Watching all the passers-by
Grockles sunbathing on the sand,
Listening to the rhythmic band.

Grey and white, great big wings,
I scour all the rubbish bins.
Now my target comes into sight,
A brilliant view from this great height.

A vanilla cone with a great big flake,
Maybe this is the one I'll take.
Spoilt for choice with lots of flavours,
Perhaps I'll steal one from their neighbours.

Down I swoop with tremendous speed,
Side-splitting with a lot of greed.
In the corner of my eye I've spied,
A lot of chips, freshly fried.

Oh well, I've already dived,
I got it and the little girl cried.
She bawled and wailed as I flew away,
With my delicious and yummy prey.

Lots more seagulls chase after me,
They are hunting for my tea.
I flap my wings lots and lots,
Until I find safety on some chimneypots.

**Emily Simons (12)**
**St Antony's Leweston School, Sherborne**

# Good Old England

Great, wet, grey country,
Pouring rain down on me,
Land of roast dinners,
The only ones that don't eat it are the sinners.

Our great Queen Lizzy II
We are the inventors of the loo,
Rolling country with sheep galore,
Cows, pigs and a whole lot more.

We won the bid to host the 2012 Olympics,
I wish they would hold the famous game, Pooh sticks,
Who's won The Ashes? *We have!*
The drawback is we seem to be having a little trouble with chavs!

We have David Beckham's right foot and Harry Potter,
I always did enjoy those books by Beatrix Potter,
Caribbean Islands, safaris . . . who needs 'em?
When I'm happy right here in good old England!

**Emma Barker  (12)**
**St Antony's Leweston School, Sherborne**


# My Best Friends

Boyfriends
Girlfriends
Kisses
Cuddles
Nothing but a messy muddle
Not for me, that mushy life
No pushy husband or bossy wife
All I need are my best friends,
They're the best for fashion trends,
We say hello and goodbye,
But we're always by each other's sides,
They like me
And I like them
And that is all that matters in the end!

**Eppie Parker  (13)**
**St Antony's Leweston School, Sherborne**

# Autumn's Come

Slowest leaf, in all its glory,
Diminished from its nurturing bough.
Reddest offspring well-nigh history,
Brown the ground for rustling now.

Torches of Heaven that radiate down,
Golden sunsets advance with speed.
Flickering out into a glowing frown,
Lessen is the shimmer to warm the leaves.

Swallows, flying angels of the sky,
Nests are empty, fledglings test their wings.
Evening's chill, eager to fly,
In pursuit of the sun; their destiny brings.

No leaves, no sun, no birds, all alone,
We remain; to await the darkening days.
Only the comfort that has been known,
Things will return, come what may.

The ice queen claims her domain,
Autumn's up, winter's in.

**Emily Margaret Rose Hewett (12)**
**St Antony's Leweston School, Sherborne**

# A Different Point Of View

I'm different, I'm original
Who wants to join the clique?
Creative and imaginative
I want to be unique!

Music that is classical -
My bow glides to the beat
Oboe concertos magical
Chromatic scales my feat.

Charging, growling goalie
No midfield dash for me
Bounding, pouncing, shooting
I then rely on thee.

Some boys, I think are farcical
I'm yet to be convinced . . .
Shopping trips just laughable
My sister says I'm jinxed.

**Tabitha Nelham Clark  (12)**
**St Antony's Leweston School, Sherborne**

# War

Soldiers, silhouetted against a painted sky,
Knocked down by a death blow fall.
Swords and armour scattered to ground,
The eeriness of silence.

The sun, a cascade of gold,
Saddened to see the crimson pools
Slithering under the warrior's feet
Into rivers dark and forgotten
Meandering slowly to their destiny.

A breath of wind carries voices,
Voices of curse,
Which sink into the sodden earth.
Souls rise,
Spirits fall,
They drift on,
Through the grasp of Hell.

**Ella Lane (12)**
**St Antony's Leweston School, Sherborne**


# The Little Spanish Town

The morning sunlight shines upon the cobbles of the Spanish street,
The people rise to greet the day with laughing eyes and dancing feet,
Above the windows of the houses coloured awnings are pulled down
And somewhere music stars to murmur in the little Spanish town.

A holiday for dancing and for drinking wine has just begun,
The dark-eyed senoritas clicking heels and swaying in the sun,
A sun whose glowing warmth and golden light
Are always there to crown,
Another day of joy and laughter in the little Spanish town.

**Louise Kingham (14)**
**St Gabriel's School, Newbury**

# That's A Degree To Love

*(Inspired by 'Twelfth Night' by Shakespeare)*

That's a degree to love,
Coming from the stars above,
Olivia speaks of her sorrows,
Towards Viola as she follows,
Through the garden, through the gate,
They walk together, as in fate.

But there is a hitch in this plan,
Olivia does not love a man,
Viola is not what she appears to be,
She is different on the inside to what people see,
For Orsino does she hold this lie,
Without him she would surely die.

Sebastian, Viola's long-lost twin,
Knows not about his living kin,
Olivia marries this handsome man,
Sebastian knows not why, but gives not a damn,
For she loves him and he loves her
And marrying Olivia he will be a 'Sir'.

Meanwhile Viola longs for her love,
Whereas Orsino still loves Olivia like a dove,
But at the end of this play,
Everyone gets their own way,
Except Malvolia who is known to be mad,
Ends up alone and is still very sad.

Sebastian and Olivia end up together,
Orsino and Viola together forever,
For Sir Toby and Maria things really work well,
For all three of these couples, chime the wedding bells,
Feste is left 'fooling' on his own
And Sir Andrew walks out of the play, all alone.

**Francesca Robertson & Katie Handley Potts  (13)**
**St Gabriel's School, Newbury**

# She Left Me Alone

Cold, alone and scared
No one there
My brother's bed empty
My mother gone
Snuggled in my covers

Floorboards creaking
Suddenly
A bang downstairs
Washing in the breeze

Then, there is a sound
It's a . . .
Key in the door
Someone saying my name
Who can it be?
*It's my mum!*
Thank goodness she's back!

**Leila Zarazel (11)**
**St Gabriel's School, Newbury**


# Lost

You are as small as a mouse,
Everything towers over you,
So many shops, too many shops
Above all the shouting and the laughing
You hear your heart . . .
*Boom, boom, boom!*
Everyone is happy, except for you,
Suddenly
You hear your name.

**Phoebe Harris (11)**
**St Gabriel's School, Newbury**

# Lost And Alone

People shouting!
Children running!
Stepping back into a dark space.

*All alone!*

Start crying!
Mum missing!
Don't know where I am.

*All alone!*

Food falling on the ground!
Shopkeepers talking!
Things breaking.

*All alone!*

I am in a cold, dark space!
All I can hear is shouting!

*I want my mum!*

**Dani Johnson  (11)**
**St Gabriel's School, Newbury**


# Lost And Found

Starting to run
Trying not to cry
People look at me
Seeing if I am alright
Palms sweating
Never-ending
Hear shouting
I can smell a perfume that's familiar
I look up
*Mum!*

**Hope Grant  (11)**
**St Gabriel's School, Newbury**

# Lost

Crowds and crowds of people
Bumping into me
Shoes slamming on the floor
I hide under a rack of clothes
Scary
Terrifying
But suddenly . . .
Something catches my eye
So I come out to find that
A hand's grabbing mine
Looking up to see
It's my grandma
Looking down with an angry face
Her expression changing
She just gives me a hug.

**Georgia Robertson (11)**
**St Gabriel's School, Newbury**

# Lost

I look around and everyone is really tall
The shopkeeper's checking and filling the shelves
I hurry down the aisle not looking where I'm walking
My heartbeat thumping in my head and racing faster
People rushing past, pushing and shoving trying to get ahead
Suddenly, there she is
My mum, at last.

**Grace Lake (11)**
**St Gabriel's School, Newbury**

# The Desert Cycle

The sun bears down,
On the dry, desert plain
And the wind stirs the sand.

The lizard watches from his rock,
The snake wriggles silently away
And a vulture pecks at its kill.

The bright blue sky shines,
Like a vast lake above the Earth
And still the day goes on and on.

A peaceful land,
A home to many
And yet so hot, but still the animals stir before the people.

A cactus lives, big by the water,
But another lives green alone
And with no other plants the land lies yellow with sand.

A scorpion hunts under the ground,
While the jackal lives above
And creatures are killed and creatures are born,
But all the while the day beats on.

The kangaroo rat scurries along,
While the ostrich runs ahead
And the sun sinks blood-red into the horizon.

The night draws in, cold but clear,
The animals come alive
And all the time around the world the people do sleep on.

A wolf spider catches his prey,
A hyena emits a cackle
And through the night the routine goes on, not stopping until dawn.

At dawn, once again, the animals retreat,
Back into their homes
And now the cycle begins again as a new day comes in the desert.

**Charlotte Thomas (11)**
**St Gabriel's School, Newbury**

# Lost

Looking round corners,
Hear people talking
And I feel 2cm tall,
But still I'm all alone.

My mum has gone,
Running up and down shop aisles
All I can see is people talking happily,
But still I'm all alone.

I'm getting pushed by people walking straight past me,
I feel like I don't exist,
I am thinking in my head, *Will she ever come back?*
Then I turn around

*Mummy!*

**Hannah Joseph  (11)**
**St Gabriel's School, Newbury**


# The School Bell

In the deep, dark corridors
Everyone towering above me
No one can see me
I feel like an ant
I can't see anyone I know
All of my friends have disappeared
And no, it can't be . . .
. . . *The bell!*
Will I be late for class?
What is my teacher going to say?
And wait . . . is that?
Yes! I've found the history room!

**Evie Harbury  (11)**
**St Gabriel's School, Newbury**

# Night Fears!

Lying in the dark,
Doors creaking,
Wind howling,
The sound of footsteps tiptoeing
Up the stairs,
I just lie wondering
What it could be,
A light turns on,
I decide to get out of bed
And see what it is,
Slowly and fearfully,
I open the door and
*Suddenly*
I find . . .
My brother!

**Jessica Townend (11)**
**St Gabriel's School, Newbury**


# Unknown Territory

Intimidated!
Shadows of fear reign your mind,
As you take every penetrating step,
Into unknown territory.

Your heart pounds like a drum,
Your stomach churns
You walk into your new school
Who knows what awaits?

**Bianca Rodriguez (11)**
**St Gabriel's School, Newbury**

# November

November glided
Through the green trees
Whispering to lime and birch
Turning each leaf to gold
Spreading the beauty of autumn
But swiftly floating on.

November pranced
By the quiet ocean
Calling to the waves
Beware December!
December is coming!

November slowed
Her pace, for autumn
Was at its end
She lingered longer
Keeping the beauty alive.

**Romala Derwent  (11)**
**St Gabriel's School, Newbury**


# Babies V Teenagers

Babies growing
Teenager's hairdryers blowing
Babies' rooms are filled with toys
Teenager's rooms are filled with boys
Babies smiling
Teenager's homework piling

Babies dribble
Teenagers scribble
Babies eat mushy peas
Teenagers eat KFCs
Babies go to playschool
Teenagers go swimming at the pool.

**Lucie Atkinson  (11)**
**St Gabriel's School, Newbury**

# Fridge Madness

A light flickers on
Someone is hungry
The chicken, wrapped in cling film
Prays that he will be chosen.

The milk, squished next to the lemonade
Wobbles in anticipation
She's about to go off
And the lemonade is hostile.

Mr Mozzarella standing
Wedged between the yoghurts
And the Dolmio pasta sauce
Awaits his turn.

The chicken kormas
Know it's not their day
They are unpopular with the other food
After all, they are packed with E numbers.

A hand reaches, but skims
Past the salad
A sigh of relief escapes from him
He lives to be digested another day.

The packaged sandwich
Gets grabbed from the far reaches
Of the top shelf
Thank goodness!
He's about to be eaten!

**Lucy Varman, Emma Bailey (14) & Kirsten Williams (13)**
**St Gabriel's School, Newbury**

# Senior School

S eeing new people coming to this school
E xciting new lessons I'll see more
N ew things to see, new places to go, new people to meet
I n the library absorbed in a book, so mysterious
O h, the bell, time for register, time for a new lesson
R eligious studies, a new room, I see a new person

S ometimes I am confused, lost within the things I've learnt
C onfused, sometimes I don't understand what we are being taught
H eading for the hills, but suddenly I understand
O ver my worries, I am understanding more the more I see
O vercome my fears I'm fine, I'm fine
L earning is something to discover.

**Natasha Hookings  (11)**
**St Gabriel's School, Newbury**


# Being New

B eing new is really scary
E verything is different
I nside I am terrified which happens really
N o one knows me
G etting used to the school now

N ot as scared as a cow at the dairy
E veryone is really friendly
W hat a good start I have made.

**Tamara McGill  (11)**
**St Gabriel's School, Newbury**

# Whispering

*Whispering,*
*Whispering.*

The silence is broken
With quiet, muffled words,
Lingering in the air,
No one knows what is being said,
Questions are being asked,
Who, what, when, where?

The whispering does many things,
Chatters, accuses, denies, exaggerates,
Recalls the shadows of past events,
Mysteries are uncovered,
As the whispering goes on.

The soft hisses are ongoing,
Showing many emotions
And spreading rumours,
Like the wind blowing long grass,
Or crickets chirping at night,
The whispering goes on.

The whispering continues,
Ears strain to catch the words,
So quiet there is hardly a sound,
Nobody can hear,
Only the maker and receiver of the words
Knows what they mean.

*Whispering,*
*Whispering,*
*Whispering.*

**Imogen Rolfe (11)**
**St Gabriel's School, Newbury**

# A New Start

At first when I walked in
I felt as if a new life was about to begin

I went to see all my old friends
Would I make some more? Well that depends

I sat at my desk, I got out my pen
When will the lesson start? *When?*

At lunch I went to play netball
Everyone else in the school was so tall

*Hooray!* It's the end of the day
But what will happen from now till May?

**Victoria Rigby (11)**
**St Gabriel's School, Newbury**

# Being New

B est friend has left
E ndless people to be your friend. My new
I nk in my bag
N ervously walking around the big, big school. A
G reat new teacher to help me along

N ear a window looking out
E ventually the bell rings. What could go
W rong on my first day at a new school?

**Lindsey Buchanan (12)**
**St Gabriel's School, Newbury**

# January

January skipped,
Through the silvery mist,
Questioning the deadly silence,
Trampling each web and melting the snowflakes,
Whispering to every tree.

January glided,
By the frozen lakes,
Looking into the impenetrable, glass-covered darkness,
Brushing the snow aside,
That settled in her path.

January pranced,
Down the hidden hills,
Stomping through the layers of frost,
Her breath a pearly white cloud,
Footprints spoiling the fast melting snow.

**Alina Rose Whitford  (11)**
St Gabriel's School, Newbury

# July

July glided
Through the shimmering ocean,
Singing to the fish,
Riding the dolphins, calling the sharks,
Smiling all the way.

July danced
Through the sunny woods,
Humming a joyful tune,
Charming both oak and fir
And trusting all the creatures.

July ran
By the flowing stream,
Whispering words of fear,
She was growing steadily older,
As August drew nearer.

**Millie Wright  (11)**
St Gabriel's School, Newbury

# The Forest

The wandering path beckons you,
Deeper and deeper into the dark.
Dead leaves crunch underfoot
And twigs snap behind me,
Under some other creatures' feet
Making me feel I am not alone.

The eerie light of the moon shines down on the forest
Bare trees sway in the fierce wind,
Their branches flex like an old man's fingers.

Then flying out from a tree, swoops a hooting owl,
As it reaches the ground, a squeal pierces the night
And the owl happily returns home.

**Milly Wiesendanger  (12)**
**St Gabriel's School, Newbury**


# My Imaginary Room

The room was multicoloured
With colours from red to blue
Big pink dots
Purple spots
Stripes, there were a lot
Orange and marine
The colour of mushy peas
The room was bright light
The multicoloured room!

**Charlotte Fowler  (11)**
**St Gabriel's School, Newbury**

# Tones

You know your own tone,
But you still dive into your bag,
Or get asked, 'Is that yours?'
You make, create, humiliate.

You can play jokes,
Ring and hang up,
You make, create, humiliate.

You make, create . . .
Different rings and tones,
Walk into a crowded place,
Let it ring,
You make, create, humiliate.

Watch people dive, hunt, rummage,
To find it's not their phone,
You make, create, humiliate.

Do it again three or four times,
Until you're caught red-handed,
*Loud* and clear,
You make, create, mistake.

**Helen Wood  (13)**
**St Gabriel's School, Newbury**


# Being New

B eginning in a new school
E verything is different
 I was scared
N evertheless excited as well
G etting new friends but still keeping old

N ew was very strange
E ven though everyone was welcoming
W hen I walked through the door, I never imagined it before.

**Melanie Davies  (11)**
**St Gabriel's School, Newbury**

# October

October shuffles
Through the colourful woods,
Rustling through the leaves,
Watching every leaf as it shakes each tree,
But never a sound made he.

October skips
In the damp woods,
Splashing through the puddles,
Watching every drop as he jumps in them,
But never a mark left he.

October sprints
In the beautiful woods,
Running through the dew,
Watching every moonlit night as he sleeps,
But never a leaf left he.

**Maddy Beckett  (12)**
**St Gabriel's School, Newbury**


# Summer

Summer danced
Along the sands
Singing to the sea
Warming the sky and warming the beach
Joyfully humming before tea

Summer flew
Through the sky
Pushing clouds away
Out came the sun
And brightened up the day

Summer lay
On the clouds
With autumn drawing near
She became much weaker
And summer was filled with fear.

**Charlotte Phelps  (11)**
**St Gabriel's School, Newbury**

# A November Winter

Winter danced
Around the snow-topped mountains,
Whispered to a squirrel,
Froze the lake and skated on the snow,
As she sang her sweet little song.

Winter crept
By the huge oak tree,
Sprayed snow and frost,
Stroked each rabbit lovingly
And then she drifted on.

Winter swayed
Across the frozen pond,
Seeking each icicle,
In her hands were snowdrops,
Treasured in her mind.

**Charlotte Osborne (11)**
**St Gabriel's School, Newbury**


# A Bauble's Dream

She stares at me,
I stare back,
My owners seem to have gone a bit over the top this year
I know this tree must look pretty,
I can hardly breathe and it's a long way down,
I stare around, left to right, right to left,
Here I am, on top of the tree, nothing can stop me.

**Louisa O'Sullivan (12)**
**St Gabriel's School, Newbury**

# Flip-Up Camera Phone

Going home from school one day
Crying because of my jealousy
'Mummy, I need some money to pay
For a flip-up camera phone.'

'Darling, I can't afford a phone,
I wish I had a better job to give you one.'
My friend has the only one and I want the clone,
It's a coloured, flip-up, camera phone.

In my school, in my class, I am the only one
Who doesn't have one or a flip-up camera phone
If I had money, it would weigh a tonne
I could buy a coloured, flip-up, camera phone.

I thought about doing extra paper rounds
To save up for my heart's desire.
I am too young; my phone is out of bounds,
I want my coloured, flip-up, camera phone!

I could wander in town on my own
If I had my fantasy mobile.
If I was in danger, I could use my precious phone,
My coloured, flip-up, camera phone.

**Joanna Weeks (13)**
**St Gabriel's School, Newbury**


# New School Days

Nervous, alone, no friends, heart thumping,
I was scared, my new school looked big and old,
I gathered my courage and went in.
I met many new girls just like me.
I didn't feel so nervous,
There is now nothing to be scared of
Or worried about.

**Fiona Muir (11)**
**St Gabriel's School, Newbury**

# December

December slipped
Silent and softly
On a shivering, bleak mountainside
Whispering only to the trees
Freezing the river and crushing each leaf
Hushing animals wherever it went.

December pounced
By the freezing wood
Hushing trees and lifting snow
Touching each flower
As it died, he moved on.

December raced
Down the mountainside
Through the snow
He made icicles as he went
Behind him was Death.

**Sophie Fowler  (11)**
**St Gabriel's School, Newbury**


# January

January drifted
Through the silent wood
Stroking owl and fox
Watering each leaf and watching each bird
And never a bad word she spoke.

January flew by the trickling stream
Hushing bird and mouse
Curing each plant silently
Whilst singing a beautiful song.

January sat
In her warm wooden hut
Dreaming happily
Outside her windows, melting snow
As new plants began to grow.

**Hannah Miles  (11)**
**St Gabriel's School, Newbury**

# Spring

Spring danced around singing,
By a wood while the brook was flowing quietly by,
Smiling sweetly with a happy voice,
She healed the animals, cured the sick,
Always cheerful deep down.

Spring skipped over the grass,
By the whispering trees,
Playing with the water and flowers,
Awakening the sleeping earth,
From its wintery sleep.

Spring raced the deer,
Through the blossoming trees,
Giggling happily as she went,
Her cheeks and lips were rosy red
And her smile as sweet as the day.

**Jennifer Ransom  (11)**
**St Gabriel's School, Newbury**


# May

Spring danced
Through the sunlit forest
Singing to lamb and plant
Loving the animals, caring for flowers
And never breaking song.

Spring rode
On her shimmering horse
Playing with rabbit and bird
Stroking every bunny lovingly
And then danced off.

Spring galloped
Over the green prairie
Laughing as she went
In her eyes was happiness
On her face was new life.

**Amy Fitzpatrick  (11)**
**St Gabriel's School, Newbury**

# A Forest Full Of Life

Lashing out
Rocking fiercely
Leafless
But yet full of life
Are the trees in the howling wind

Crunching
Snapping
Hard and lumpy
The twigs underfoot

Twitching
Dry old leather
Pinprick eyes upside down
And a high-pitched noise
The bats in the treetops.

Cold
Damp dew
The sun has gone
Replaced by the full moon
Werewolves barking
Night falls on the eerie forest
Like a widow's veil.

**Annabel Hawkesworth (12)**
**St Gabriel's School, Newbury**


# The Forest

The rays of sunshine through the opening of the treetops
Bumblebees buzzing from flower to flower
Birds collecting twigs to start a new family
The blanket of bluebells paints the forest
The soft winding stream glitters with delight
The orchestra of birds never stops singing
The deer dance with happiness, hurdling the fallen branches
Rabbits have tea parties down in their burrows.

**Rebecca Bowen (13)**
**St Gabriel's School, Newbury**

# Being New At School

B eastly feeling in my stomach
E normous headache that just won't go
I n the playground, everyone's staring at me
N o one to play with, my best friend is gone but suddenly
G irls are coming up to me and chatting with me

N ow the lessons start and we have to work in pairs
E veryone wants to be my partner but I choose Tash
W ell, maybe being new is not so bad after all

A t home this morning it seemed like everything would go wrong
T hough I've made lots of friends and everything is fine

S chool is almost over and I have had a *great* day
C oming back tomorrow seems *soooo* far away
H ome time is only a minute to go
O odles to tell my mum and dad
O h, I can't wait for tomorrow to come
L eaving school is really sad.

**Katherine Gedeon  (11)**
**St Gabriel's School, Newbury**


# The Great Big Senior School

At first I felt I didn't belong
Until my best friends came along.

The senior school is very scary
It makes me feel as small as a fairy.

The first weeks have gone by very fast,
I like the senior school finally, at last.

The senior school is really fun,
The start of the year has just begun.

Now I think the school is great,
Tomorrow's a new day and I can't wait!

**Sarah Goble  (11)**
**St Gabriel's School, Newbury**

# School

Dark creeps across the sky,
Howling winds grab at the swaying trees,
Gates creek, doors bang,
The noise of engines starting up, but a car nowhere to be seen,
Running footsteps crunch against the stones,
But never come closer,
The lights click on, lighting up the playground,
Shadows growing up the walls,
Someone's fingers being dragged down a blackboard,
A scream,
But no one around,
All alone on the playground.

**Kerry Mitchell (12)**
**St Gabriel's School, Newbury**


# Graveyard

Creeping vines stick to the headstone of a dark, eerie grave,
Church wall bears down on the silent graveyard,
The wind screams in your ear as you dare to walk
Along the death-stricken path,
The statues shadow over you as you stand mourning
For your loved one,
Trees sway, acting like the Devil possesses them,
The moonlight hits the graves and illuminates them,
Bats screech as they sit watching you from their perch,
Sounds of the trees make goosebumps climb up your arm,
You feel alone as the darkness swallows you.

**Lucy Scott (13)**
**St Gabriel's School, Newbury**

# She Looks

She looks
Into me, into I
I don't know why
The others show a happy face
In this dark and deserted place.

She stares
Into me, into I
I don't know why
I see in her, a long-lost love
A need from those above.

She believes
In me, in I
I don't know why
I see her in a patchwork quilt
Filled with memories of guilt.

She knows
It is me, it is I
Flying from distant skies
I see in her a loving need
To share the load, she starts to bleed.

She cries
For me, for I
I now know why
I see in her a dark, dull face
Carrying an everlasting sadness.

She screams
In front of me, in front of I
I am sure I know why
She cries her goodbyes
As they take her away to die.

**Adrienne Hardwick  (12)**
**St Gabriel's School, Newbury**

# Don't Disappear

Furry, fluffy
Cute and cuddly
Loveable and sweet

I see you on your scratch post
Or running about outside
You may be a cat
But you've a heart of gold inside

I hate to have a favourite
I hate to have just one
But I've got to admit
I have lots of fun

I love you a lot
Now I love you even more
But going on holiday
Will be quite a bore

I guess I'll send postcards
I'll buy souvenirs
I know you'll miss me
I know there'll be tears

I love you a lot
So don't disappear!

**Jenna Sabine  (13)**
**St Gabriel's School, Newbury**

# What's Love?

The feeling for your mother,
Father, sister or brother?
For friends?
Partners?
How can we know the real meaning of love?

When do we know that it's more than just a crush?
Into something more,
What?
Love?
Will we feel it in our hearts?

When we say those words, 'I love you,' what do we mean?
Love as a friend,
Or more?
And how can we know what is right?

When we walk down the aisle and say, 'I do,'
Do we mean, 'I love you'?
Or simply, 'I do'?

How long will our perfect world last?
Days?
Weeks?
Months?
Years?
Or forever?

**Charlotte Garner  (13)**
**St Gabriel's School, Newbury**

# Come And Gone

He glances at me,
*Ka-thump, ka-thump,*
Oh no, he's coming towards me,
*Ka-thump, ka-thump.*

Just asked for my number,
*Ka-thump, ka-thump,*
Talking, dancing,
*Ka-thump, ka-thump.*

Left with my friend,
*Thump, thump, ka-thump,*
A text,
*Ka-thump, thump,*
Feeling has come, feeling gone,
*Thump, thump!*

**Olivia McCarthy (13)**
**St Gabriel's School, Newbury**


# No Love!

I'm swinging solo,
Without a single care,
I'm not intending
And I never shall,
My heart is full,
Only for fun and games,
I'm swinging solo,
Without a care!

**Lottie Crocker (13)**
**St Gabriel's School, Newbury**

# Moss

One wet nose pushes at my hands,
I turn around and there stands
A beautiful face, gazing at me,
Tongue licking like crazy; that's what I see,
One ear up, one ear down, so silky to touch,
Tail up, wagging so much.

This is our latest family member,
Her name is Moss, she arrived in September,
She is incredibly pretty and so, so fit,
We have taught her to stay, come and sit,
She can chase after everything, especially a ball
And she's absolutely brilliant at the recall.

Whatever happens and whatever we detest,
Moss is our dog and she is the best!

**Clare Warwick (13)**
**St Gabriel's School, Newbury**


# My True Love

His blue eyes are blinding,
They keep me smiling,
Through wind and rain,
They will always be the same.

His body is lush,
It always makes me blush,
His hair is blond,
Along with a body like James Bond!

I love his smile,
It always lasts a while,
It will even last for years.

He keeps me happy
And makes me feel lucky!

**Emily Woods (13)**
**St Gabriel's School, Newbury**

# Love Of My Life

Roses are red
Violets are blue
I know in my heart
I really love you

I'm not much good at writing
So please excuse me
But I was just hoping
That you'd come with me

We'll go out to dinner
Wherever you want
We'll have lots of champagne
Well, that's what I'd hoped

But if you say no
I'll go back home
And a watch a love video
All on my own.

**Siena Hatton-Brown  (13)**
**St Gabriel's School, Newbury**


# Graveyard

As the jet-black night dawns,
An owl shrieks at its furry prey,
Swooping, hunting, needing to be fed,
Squawking with every flap of its wings.

The trees crack and overhang the shadow-struck churchyard,
Shivering, rustling as they're so bare,
No leaves to keep them warm,
On the piercing winter nights.

Paths fracture with every foot laid upon them,
Rivers of tears crack the edges,
Leaves scatter, covering the yard.

**Hannah Bown  (13)**
**St Gabriel's School, Newbury**

# Precious Possessions

*(In the style of Kit Wright)*

My box is platinum,
It's precious to me,
Inside it contains things only I can see:

A frothy hot chocolate,
The warmth of the sun
And the aroma of a bubbly cappuccino.

The smile of a baby,
The squidgy sand between my toes,
The smell of my mother's perfume.

The whisper of crunching snow,
The love of snuggling with my fluffy dog,
The thrill of a galloping roller coaster.

These may seem strange to you,
But to me they will stay in my heart,
*Forever!*

**Joanna Ash (12)**
**St Gabriel's School, Newbury**


# Summer

Gliding smoothly through the woods,
One foot green, one blue,
She lives in the air all around us.
Giving warm hugs all the time,
Her hair golden with loopy curls,
Unwinding down from Heaven,
Someone falls, Summer will catch,
Someone cries, Summer will heal.
She is a loving mother,
Her eyes are made of fresh flowers,
She brings the key to brighten up the world!

**Kiran Bhusate (12)**
**St Gabriel's School, Newbury**

# Having Tied Feet

All there is, is immense pain,
I've always walked so slow.
Hobbling and swaying,
Because it is the fashion.
Crushing my arch,
My crippled feet,
I could never sleep.
I screamed with pain and despair,
But no one came,
They didn't care.
Deformed all my life,
I hate it, I do.
I would wish this on no one,
Though someone wished this on me!

**Letitia Rizan  (12)**
**St Gabriel's School, Newbury**


# To And Fro

I see a night's sky,
Stars running by,
Calm, cool, countryside,
Fields and mountains too,
Hedges dotting the land.

People all over the place waving to and fro,
Drifting trees, crispy bacon and sausages on the BBQ,
The warm, tender glow of people waving to and fro.

The frost on a cold winter's night,
The waft of bacon wavering to and fro.

**Amelia Richardson  (12)**
**St Gabriel's School, Newbury**

# Trophy

I came home happy, I shouted to my mum,
'I've got it, I can see myself.'
I looked back at the trophy and I lost it, my face had gone.
I relaxed and saw myself once more,
All round, my nose bigger than my eyes.
I walked round the house looking at the deformed shapes
Of my room, my teddies, the stairs.
Then I saw my mum
I walked towards her, my eyes still on the trophy.

As she looked at me, I looked straight back
But she didn't see me, she saw herself.
I felt disappointed.
When she took me and looked at me
I saw her and I thought she saw me
But I was wrong.

As I looked at my mum through the trophy
I saw something else, I didn't know what
But I sensed sadness, something locked away
My mum looked at me and tapped me on the shoulder
But I couldn't bring my eyes from the sad face of the trophy.

**Suzanne Hocking  (12)**
**St Gabriel's School, Newbury**


# Socks

These are the socks
Bought new in Scotland
These are the socks
Keeping me warm on walks
These are the socks
I wear in bed
These are the socks
Comfy in my wellies
These are the socks
That I wore in my wellies
On the hills in Scotland.

**Georgia Benney  (11)**
**St Gabriel's School, Newbury**

# Summer

Luminous sun,
Reflecting on the radiant turquoise sea,
Swimming and snorkelling,
All day long.

Happy and bouncy,
Willing to talk,
Young girls and boys,
Having beach parties.

Pale clothing to keep cool,
Slapping suncream on,
Designer shades for protection,
In the warm Hollywood sun.

Strutting her stuff,
Showing off,
Her tanned legs
And her curvaceous body.

Her thick blonde hair,
Swaying in the sea breeze,
Sunbathing in her bikini,
Topping up her tan.

**Georgia Hawkesworth (12)**
St Gabriel's School, Newbury

# Ode To A Grass Snake

Oh lithesome snake, don't choose to sleep,
In the secret depths of our compost heap.
It may be dark and warm and dry,
But beware the fork that dares to pry.
I fear that in the end you must,
End your life as rich hummus!

**Lucy Meredith (11)**
St Gabriel's School, Newbury

# Splish, Splash, Splosh

On with the wellies
And out we go.
I wonder where.
*Splish, splash, splosh.*
 We arrive
There are loads of children
Running here, running there.
*Splish, splash, splosh.*
Mum is sitting down reading her book,
Why don't grown-ups join in the fun too?
*Splish, splash, splosh.*
Anticipation makes me anxious,
Laughter and playfulness awaits me.
*Splish, splash, splosh.*
Finally, it's time to leave
Disappointment hits me like a big bomb
But I will come back another day.
I will, I will.
*Splish, splash, splosh!*

**Rhianna MacGregor (12)**
**St Gabriel's School, Newbury**

# Being New

I was standing nervously
At the door
Of my new school
I took a deep breath
And reached for the handle
As I stepped inside
Warm faces welcomed me
To a new beginning.

**Ellie Baxter (11)**
**St Gabriel's School, Newbury**

# A Girl's Head

In it there is a room filled with people
And my duvet for a poem in English!

And there is
The class,
Which shall be next?

And there is an entirely new flower,
An entirely new person,
An entirely new key

There is a lock to an unknown room.

There is an ink eradicator

There is a mark

And it will not erase

I believe
What cannot be erased
Is a memory.

There is much promise
In the circumstance
That so many people have memories.

**Francesca Tennant (13)**
**Sherborne School for Girls, Sherborne**


# Gothic Poem

T he catching and fearing of each sound
H ow the horror filled the angry hall
O vercoming this was impossible
R eflecting rainfall damaged the roof
N obody knew what fear I was in
F ear followed me through the freezing school halls
I ntense stress flowed through my blood
E nhancing the extinguishing noises
L ights flashed in a daunting way
D eath . . .

**Rachael Ellis (13)**
**Sherborne School for Girls, Sherborne**

*Young Writers - POP! Southern England*

# A Girl's Head

There are galloping horses that never stop.

There is fear.

There is a crowded place, lost with the people in it.

There is hate, but it is not known what for.

There is sadness, for growing.

But there is always joy for the sun shining through the windows.

There is a sun, a jungle and two friends
Who vanished without a trace.

There are butterflies.

There is hunger.

There are things wanted.

There is want for love and happiness.

But the heart never comes to the head,
So some things just die and fade away in the end.

**Emily Rainbow  (13)**
**Sherborne School for Girls, Sherborne**


# Gothic Poem

T he lightning pelted into the vast dark sky
H orror struck the poor man's eye
O ther shadows flickered through the moonlight
R unning away, into the night
N o one dared care, no one dared pity
F og rolled over the city
I nto the houses, the weak figure ran
E ndless crying out for this man
L ittle cries could be heard throughout the night
D eadly signs showed, it would not be alright.

**Georgina Bolton Carter  (13)**
**Sherborne School for Girls, Sherborne**

# A Gothic Poem

T he rain seemed unstoppable as it beat against the window
H owever, the sun shone clearly through. To the west was a
     wonderful array of colours, forming a sparkling rainbow
O ur moods were similar
R estless with excitement as we had just become engaged
N onetheless we remained calm and watched the gardener as he
F etched his penknife as if he was about to fulfil his daily chore
     of cutting open the netting which covered the new hay bales
I t blazed as it reflected the dazzling sunlight, I knew immediately
    as he made a sudden movement towards the young man that the
E nd was coming for the young stable boy, Edward
L ong had the gardener despised the child, who now lay
D esperately in pain and within a few seconds he had gone still
     and slowly all evidence of vividness drained out of him and the
       colour in his rosy cheeks faded away as if a leech were
         sucking away his blood. Edward was dead.

**Pippa Jenkins  (13)**
**Sherborne School for Girls, Sherborne**


# Thornfield Hall Sonnet

T owering high, a fortress of despair
H idden here behind the crumbling dark walls
O vergrown and waiting for its true heir
R evealing the dark secret in its halls
N othing comes nearby when that scream emits
F leeting shadows unmask his frightful fate
I nsane is she as she falls into fits
E very laugh shrill and bleak breeds fear and hate
L ittle time now does the master spend here
D usty and empty stands the old mansion

H e comes, but is soon overcome by fear
A ll thoughts come back, he hides in submission
L ife has forsaken this sorrowful place
L unacy rules from that contorted face.

**Chloë E Scott  (13)**
**Sherborne School for Girls, Sherborne**

# Butterfly

Alone I stand,
My tender arms hang limp by my side,
As I draw the knife across my untouched flesh.

A blood-red flower blooms,
A perfect imperfection.
So beautiful, I panic as it trickles away
And weaves down fast into the sink.

Tears burn my eyes like acid,
I cannot hold on to my vulnerability,
My open wound.

All emotions released like Pandora's box.

The blood butterfly flies freely in the sink,
Yet it begins to drown in the sea of despair.
Its wings snap and its body shivers,
From the sweeping insensitivity of this world.

My cries hushed by the wind,
Silence stills the room.
Stillness that heaves, swells and overpowers.

Peaceful and alone, I fall.
You tore off my wings.

**Georgia Horrocks  (14)**
**Sherborne School for Girls, Sherborne**


# Death

D eath
E very voice I hear reminds me of her
A deadly silence clouding over me
T he only friend I had who will never come back
H e took her away, but I shall never forget her.

**Alice Hayes  (13)**
**Sherborne School for Girls, Sherborne**

# Gothic Poem

T otal silence, nothing stirring
H orror racks the brain as footsteps approach
O ut of the silence of the night emerges a shattering scream
R aging rain beats the large glass panes harshly
N ow the steps cease and incomprehension washes over me
F rozen to the spot I am surrounded by my reflections
                              as mirrors confirm my situation
I n the grate the fire flickers, nervously
E ncouraged by my imagination my thoughts are of ghosts
                                            and monsters

L eaving these behind I know I must proceed
D own the hallway stairs I slide, silent as a ghost

H earing the piercing screams again I stop motionless
A lways glancing behind I follow the distressed screeching
L amenting the happy times I used to know, that I know would
                                        never be the same again
L osing the feeling in my fingers as I reach to prise open
                                            the dreaded door.

**Natasha Marks (13)**
**Sherborne School for Girls, Sherborne**


# A Gothic Poem

T he grave lit up with a flash of light
H orrific thoughts filled my pounding head
O ver there, a movement, a flash
R ays of light glistened on the only white tombstone in the graveyard
N ancy Rims was the name scratched on the tombstone
F lashing light filled my head illuminating the gloomy sky
I n a crack the tombstone split
E verything in my body froze
L it up from the light, a creature emerged from the ground
                                        dressed all in black
D read and hate filled my head, I had been expecting this for years.

**Alice Maltby (13)**
**Sherborne School for Girls, Sherborne**

# Gothic Poem

T all, twisting thorn trees surround the mysterious castle
H ollow loneliness fills every gloomy corridor, hall and room
O minous sounds rattle through the ghostly manor
R ain outside steams the windows as the wind howls a tune
N ight has arrived at Thornfield Hall inviting with it a
thunderous storm
F aint footsteps echo within the silent old walls
I nner doors are locked and with them secrets from the past
are carefully hidden
E verything dares not stir, nothing is heard except for the
ghostly creaking of the tall, black, swinging gates
L ightning tears down a page of darkness, illuminating a row
of thorny figures, twisting their jagged arms towards the skies
D arkness once again envelops the world around the large estate

H igh within the castle, a villainous laugh erupts from one of the
hidden chambers
A ll is once again still
L ittle by little the storm starts to roll away
L onely twilight peeps through the curtain of darkness, as if to
signify the approach of day.

**Antonia Hollis (13)**
**Sherborne School for Girls, Sherborne**


# Thornfield

T he blanket of the dark washed over me
H orror trembled down my spine
O paque was my thought, opaque was my mind
R igidity reigned my body and soul
N ow the thunder echoed through my mind
F reak lightning shattered across the sky like a bag of marbles
splitting into the heavens.
I n the bleakness of the night there arose a terrifying cry
E nding the silence of the starry sky
L ight rays playing across the white walls
D ozing off I heard a cackling peal of laughter . . .

**Louise Crowley (13)**
**Sherborne School for Girls, Sherborne**

# My Night In The Woods

T he dreary night loomed on

H orror filled my body as the murderer approached me

O h, for now he held out his hand to place around my mouth

R unning away from him my mind was panicking

N erves of steel now were not so strong

F rightened and afraid I kept on going for my heart was
                              pounding like the beat of African drums

I n time I lay low and I was so close to the ground that I
                              could hear the footsteps of my killer

E dging closer to being exhausted I tried to keep on running

L ife, I now saw my dear, loving family and friends standing
                                                      there before me

D ead, he had found me.

**Tessa Astbury  (14)**
**Sherborne School for Girls, Sherborne**


# Gothic Poem

T hreatening noises

H aunted corridors

O minous master

R aving anger

N auseous making

F ire in the bedroom

I solated house

E erie noises

L aughter in the attic

D eath of hopes.

**Elizabeth Norman  (13)**
**Sherborne School for Girls, Sherborne**

# Marine Life

I dive deeper, under the sea,
The pressure building in my ears,
I can see many fish, swimming all around me,
*Glub, glib, glob.*
They release air bubbles, floating to the surface,
I swim deeper and see a wreck,
An old ship, far past its former glory,
Seaweed binds it to the seabed, waving up and down,
*Wibble, wobble, stretch.*
Fish and coral at its hull,
Silently guarding the hidden treasure,
The ship creaking its protest,
Hidden behind splinters of wood,
*Creak, crack, splinter.*
The fish flee, as I turn sharply,
To a noise from a team member,
They have found gold
And scatter it, in their joy,
*Cling, sprinkle, slap.*
But now I check my air tank; it is nearly empty,
I regret that I must go now,
From this underwater paradise,
Back to the surface, and the real world,
*Glub, glib, glob.*
The water washes off my head, my hair drooping,
And the memories seem to flood out of my mind
For now, maybe to come back at a later time,
Goodbye, my secret heaven.

**Thomas Starling (12)**
**Sir Joseph Williamson Mathematical School, Rochester**

# Punch And Judy

Immense power
Dangerous fixation
Unaware puppet
Or hazardous imbecile

Never-ending
Oblivious for the lack of aptitude
A lucky nation
Passing the turmoil

Father's war
Attempting to impress
The finger of blame is passed
To undeserved victims

The puppet man hides
No feeling of guilt
Untiring destruction
The blood on his hands
The blood on his hands.

**Ben Shrubsole  (15)**
**Sir Joseph Williamson Mathematical School, Rochester**


# Autumn

As soon as the first leaf falls
Summer is retreating
When the wind calls
The birds are fleeting

As the sun lowers
Heating bills rise
The end for mowers
But not the lies

Autumn is vulnerable
Where it sits . . .

**James Tutt  (13)**
**Sir Joseph Williamson Mathematical School, Rochester**

# Hallowe'en

Hallowe'en is the night
The night for fright
All the children dressing up as ghouls and ghosts
The night for fright
Bobbing for apples and other party games
The night for fright
Pumpkins keep it all alight
The night for fright

Hallowe'en is the night
The night for fright
The witches ride upon their broomsticks
The night for fright
Ghosts and ghouls come back to life
The night for fright
All to fade away at the stroke of midnight
The night for fright.

**Tommy Nundy  (13)**
**Sir Joseph Williamson Mathematical School, Rochester**


# The Kestrel

I am quick yet steady,
Silent and swift;
I may be small, but I am deadly.
I have a sharp eye;
To hunt for my prey,
I hover, patiently waiting;
Then, using my stealth,
I catch it with a grip of steel;
From my iron claws,
I resist its struggle
And with my razor-like beak,
I turn it into my next meal.

**Ben Stroud  (12)**
**Sir Joseph Williamson Mathematical School, Rochester**

# The Seasons

*(Dedicated to my mum, dad and sister who have been so supportive of me)*

The cold and the icy wind ran rapidly round my ears
The cold and the icy wind froze my little tears.

The cold and the icy snow came down from the heavens above
The cold and the icy snow flew like a little dove.

The cold and the icy windmill creaked as its long arms turned
The cold and the icy windmill fell as its wood was burned.

Wind and snow and hail came
The seasons turned once again.

The bright and rain-covered tulips were budding for the spring
The bright and rain-covered tulips were regal like a king.

The bright and rain-covered robins were singing in their nest
The bright and rain-covered robins with their little glowing red breast.

The bright and rain-covered chickens were laying eggs again
The bright and rain-covered chickens were laying in lots of ten.

Blossom, sun and breeze came
The seasons turned again.

The scorched and red-hot beaches were full to the brim
The scorched and red-hot beaches were golden like a pin.

The scorched and red-hot burgers were cooking on the grill
The scorched and red-hot burgers had hungry stomachs to fill.

The scorched and red-hot children got out of school
The scorched and red-hot children dived in the swimming pool.

Burned ribs and hot dogs came
The seasons turned again.

The shivering, coloured leaves blew in the wind
The shivering, coloured leaves, none an identical twin.

The shivering, coloured fires heated all the house
The shivering, coloured fires twitched like a mouse.

The shivering, coloured fireworks whizzed round the sky
The shivering, coloured fireworks and home-baked apple pie.

**Matthew Roberts  (12)**
**Sir Joseph Williamson Mathematical School, Rochester**

# Sir Lancelot

*(Inspired by 'The Lady of Shalott' by Alfred, Lord Tennyson)*

One gloomy night Sir Lancelot gazed,
At several stars at whom he praised,
To a lady that lived in Camelot,
The Lady of Shalott.

So riding down his war horse came,
He might have thought it was a game.
But soon they came beside a river,
As a cold wind made him quiver.

And then he saw a pale face,
That disappeared without a trace,
He ran inside a battered barn
And saw within a silver yarn.

He liked the girl that had disappeared,
He thought he was going to be killed, he feared,
He found her in a flood of tears,
I will curse you, she hears.

This was a witch, a powerful one,
A terrible crime she had done.
To curse a beautiful girl so young,
A spell that should be undone.
The Lady of Shalott.

**Alex Brown  (11)**
**Sir Joseph Williamson Mathematical School, Rochester**

# Sir Lancelot

*(Inspired by 'The Lady of Shalott' by Alfred, Lord Tennyson)*

He wrote a letter
To his love
In the middle of the night
And sent out a white dove

As he wrote his love letter
He was determined
With all his might
He would get her

Lancelot stood there
Tall and lanky
And waited for a maid
To bring his hanky

He galloped towards Shalott
On his horse
To go and save . . .
The Lady of course

The Lady took a boat from the river
And started rowing
Down the stream
As night fell, she began to shiver

Lancelot wouldn't give up
Or stop
The Lady was cold
And her body began to drop

His horse slowed down
And then it bled
The boat drifted over
And he realised his fear . . .
The Lady of Shalott was dead

There he was stranded
So he took out his knife
Cut himself
And threw away his life.

**Sam Brown (11)**
**Sir Joseph Williamson Mathematical School, Rochester**

# Sir Lancelot Poem

*(Inspired by 'The Lady of Shalott' by Alfred, Lord Tennyson)*

On the side of the river,
Sir Lancelot cried,
Laying down with a shiver
Waiting for his bride
The Lady of Shalott.

Then she came,
With a smile,
Lancelot called her name,
She was carrying a file,
The Lady of Shalott.

Blood on the floor,
Sir Lancelot went,
No life, no more,
Back to his tent,
The Lady of Shalott.

**Sam Pepper (11)**
**Sir Joseph Williamson Mathematical School, Rochester**

# Polar Bear

I'm sometimes on my own out in the cold,
I'm really white and really quite bold,
I start the day with a big helping of fish
And eat with my hands, without a dish.

I protect my young with all my life,
Especially from people with a knife,
My big bold body gives people a fright,
Especially when they see me in the night.

**Jack Poynter (12)**
**Sir Joseph Williamson Mathematical School, Rochester**

# Protest

The increasing loudness of a protest, marching like an army
The people on the pavement think they're all barmy
The stomping, the stamping crashing down to earth in anger.

Viewers watch like hypnotised zombies frozen in space
Robotic protestors jolt their boards up and down in an even pace
The boards, bold as brass, are coloured like a fluorescent rainbow.

The roaring and raging of voices carries through the air
Bringing people to come and stop and stare
The protest moves along as a heavy steam carriage
And starts to fade.

The stomping, the stamping of feet
The swish, the wish of boards
The roaring, the raging of voices
The silence of the street.

**Jonathan Nunn  (12)**
**Sir Joseph Williamson Mathematical School, Rochester**


# Warrior

The shiny swirls engraved upon the hilt
Flash wildly as metal strikes metal
A conflict deciding life and death,
Separating the strong from the weak.
A sudden blow snatches away a life,
Never to return to the world of the living.
But another fights on,
For he shall not fall -
His instrument of death has never let him down,
Nor has his trusty steed,
Nor his nerve of steel.
For this is the saviour - the only hope
For this bleak and desolate land
For this is the warrior.
The warrior.

**Samuel Seed  (11)**
**Sir Joseph Williamson Mathematical School, Rochester**

# Swimming Pool

Holidaymakers,
Lying on the sunbed
Soaking up the sun
Until they go red.

Chlorine in the water
Stinging my eyes.
My mum's temper
Is starting to rise.

Jumping in the pool
Making a splash,
My little sister jumps in,
Giving me a bash.

Smell of the barbecue,
Just around the corner.
When I get there,
It's as hot as a sauna.

Children screaming
Hurting my ears,
Feels like it has been
Going on for years.

The lifeguard
Is whistling to warn,
The constant trilling
Is making me yawn.

**Jamie Cogle (11)**
**Sir Joseph Williamson Mathematical School, Rochester**

# Seasons A Whole Year Around

A white blanket covers the land
The trees are stripped of their foliage
And the wind howls in its lonesomeness.
It seems that time is at a standstill
With this ice age ruling on for centuries
But there is hope.
The dawn breaks and winter will be a lost memory
Carried by the wind
The glow of light warms the desolate land that awakens the Earth
The breath of life brings a leap of rejuvenation.
Once again, the trees are newly clothed in their foliage
And the Earth sings a chorus of new life and an everlasting
Rush of ecstasy through the veins of all that live.
The breath turns into summer in all its power and glory
And reveals its true nature
It seems that the newfound power was not so forgiving after all.
A breath of heat rains down mercilessly
Famine cracks the whip on the Earth
As the people cry out for mercy.
Their prayers have been answered as the breath dies
And the land is a festival of brown, orange and yellow
But what they had wished for has turned against them
As the ice age begins again.
So, the people are all asleep and sound,
None can avoid the seasons a whole year around.

**Kyle Hellemans (12)**
**Sir Joseph Williamson Mathematical School, Rochester**

# The Battleground

The war begins
In the morning sun
The troops marching
The vultures perching

Rifles smoking
Men hoping
The war will end soon
Or they will all be at their doom!

Machine guns chattering
Grenades are clattering
I can smell the gunpowder
Can it get any louder?

Rifles smoking
Men hoping
The war will end soon
Or they will all be at their doom!

The rolling of tanks
The bullets clank
The missile screeches
While the medic reaches

Rifles smoking
Men hoping
The war will end soon
Or they will all be at their doom!

**Matthew Maybury (11)**
**Sir Joseph Williamson Mathematical School, Rochester**

# A Song
*(Inspired by 'The Lady of Shalott' by Alfred, Lord Tennyson)*

As we were reaping
We heard a song leaping
As it travelled
It was unravelled
As sung by the Lady of Shalott
The swaying barley
Danced joyfully
As sung by the Lady of Shalott.

Every day we heard her song
Beautiful and long
In harmony with the splashing
Of the river mashing
As sung by the Lady of Shalott
Until we heard no more of her dreaming
No more beautiful singing
By the Lady of Shalott.

**Andrew Fenton  (11)**
**Sir Joseph Williamson Mathematical School, Rochester**

# Holiday

The farmer says I'm going on holiday;
I hope it's to a far-flung bay.
He says I'll enjoy it
And get over my habit
Of eating all the green, green grass
And annoying all the top brass.
The farmer told me where I'm going;
I hope I'm going on a Boeing,
Shooting down the runway tar
I wonder, where is abattoir?

Pig.

**Andrew Bowdery  (13)**
**Sir Joseph Williamson Mathematical School, Rochester**

# West End And Broadway

The lights are flashing,
The taxis are dashing.
Fish shops are frying,
People are buying.

Babies cry,
Mothers sigh.

Stars' names up in lights!
The neon glow in the night.
Christmas specials, The Lion King,
'Chitty Chitty Bang Bang' we all sing!

The underground is roaring;
The birds are soaring.

Ice creams are melting,
Hailstones are pelting.
Tired people begin to nap,
Babies lying on mothers' laps.

Getting to the end of the day,
By the harbour, near the bay.

**Krishna Joshi  (11)**
**Sir Joseph Williamson Mathematical School, Rochester**

# Autumn Falls

In the autumn
The trees start to die.
The leaves hang loose
On a piece of string.
All crinkly and brown
And when it feels right,
They get cut.
They fall to the ground,
With no sound at all.

**Ben Wellard  (11)**
**Sir Joseph Williamson Mathematical School, Rochester**

# A Shark

I am free
I swim in deep water
I am intelligent
I rule the sea.

I am a predator;
I have three rows of pointy teeth.
I am feared!
I have rough and tough skin, pitted with scars.

I am determined;
I have eyes the size of ping-pong balls.
I am large;
I have grey skin.

What am I?

*I am a shark!*

**Daniel Barker  (11)**
**Sir Joseph Williamson Mathematical School, Rochester**


# Sparrowhawk

I am the predator,
Swifter than the wind.

I am silent but alert
And protective over my young.

I am discreet,
As I hover patiently;

I am agile and streamlined,
As I attack with talons of steel.

I am small,
But quick-witted and beady-eyed.

I am carefree as I dart through dense woodland,
And soar over open plains.

I am the sparrowhawk.

**Callum Burgess  (12)**
**Sir Joseph Williamson Mathematical School, Rochester**

# Hallowe'en

At 6pm as I look out on the street,
My head starts to boil, I get cold feet.
My body shivers, my teeth chatter,
What's happening here, what is the matter?
Hallowe'en, it is today!
Holy cow! I must hide away.
The people out there are turning grim,
Those who are cheerful, end up dim.
An era of darkness has finally commenced,
We are becoming so stupid and lack common sense.
I'm starting to see such frightening creatures,
I'm startled, stunned by their terrifying features.
Ghouls, ghosts, gremlins and witches,
We've all gone to hide in cellars and ditches.
What will happen now? I do not know,
But Christmas is near, I hope it will snow!

**James Spencer (13)**
**Sir Joseph Williamson Mathematical School, Rochester**


# Sly Spider In Waiting

Scuttling slowly across the branches of an aged tree,
I construct my invisible ambush for the carefree flies.
They have no time to realise,
That they are heading straight into the heart
Of my cunning contraption.
As the fly becomes my victim, it struggles and squirms,
Whilst I advance, coating it in a layer of sticky, silken thread.
I leave my captive, after injecting it with my venom,
To die slowly as the poison immobilises its body,
Rendering it helpless and unable to escape its inevitable fate.
Later I will return,
And eradicate the juices from the insides of the victim,
Leaving a useless shell of a body to decompose and rot.

**Victor Williams (14)**
**Sir Joseph Williamson Mathematical School, Rochester**

# Fire Fool

On a fine Sunday morning,
A boy called Ben was bored;
So his dad read him a book,
But all the way through he snored.

He had the idea of matches,
So sent his kind dad away,
'Don't play with them, it's dangerous.'
But that Ben did not obey.

He lit a match, then two and three
And oh, he was having such joy,
Lighting them in turn in the shed,
Oh, what a silly little boy!

He got very close to the fireworks,
Dancing an excited jig;
He struck a match in little jerks,
It went up like an oil rig.

The explosion was hideously loud,
Some say that it went *whack*.
Up came a mushroom cloud . . .
And the little boy turned black.

So listen up kids and take heed:
Don't play with fire for a laugh,
But instead just go and read
Or perhaps a luxurious, cosy bath . . .
*And don't do it!*

**Joel Calder (13)**
**Sir Joseph Williamson Mathematical School, Rochester**

# Bonfire Night

Fire's burning,
Rocket's soaring,
Flying up high,
Children screaming,
With delight.
Bangs, scuttles,
Through the air at midnight.
Colours shine in the damp sky,
Illuminating the crowds
And the silent cities below.
Sparklers shimmering
Incandescent
Catherine wheels screeching
And spraying their sparkling tails
Across the crowd,
Their energy slowly depleting,
Draining,
As they eventually stop
And fizzle out.
Scarecrows of the Guy,
Being savagely thrown upon the fire;
Slowly it licks the ragged scarecrows
And soon engulfs them in its heat and maliciousness.
The wonders of heat and flame,
Colour and light.
These are the wonders of Bonfire Night!

**Edward Brookes (13)**
**Sir Joseph Williamson Mathematical School, Rochester**

# Thinking What To Write

*I sat at my desk, thinking what to write.*
Then, a three-headed dragon crashed through the window!
It didn't breathe fire though, it sprayed spiked crystals from its mouth.
They were flying at me with perfect accuracy and seemed
                                                sure to hit . . .

*That's good. I'll write that down.*
However, I was distracted by the gnome who magically appeared.
He was dancing a hypnotic spell, like a cunning professional.
He took me under my bed, to reveal a passageway of corridors.
I walked and walked, until I came to an astounding door of light . . .

*I wish. That'll sound cool, though.*
But there was more to come, for I looked out of my window,
To learn that Canada had taken over all of Rochester!
An army marched down the roads, destroying anyone that got
                                                in their way.

They showed no mercy, left no survivors,
(Showed everyone how to play hockey, the *hard* way).
Suddenly, a mass of dread reached my heart, I didn't want to die,
My future looked bleak, my hope destroyed . . .

*My mind is messed, I need to take pills.*

**Adam Owen  (14)**
**Sir Joseph Williamson Mathematical School, Rochester**


# Sam's Fear

Good old Sam was a wonderful man, but the weirdest life had he
He did not sleep, not even a peep, for the morning he wanted to see
In the heart of the night, he thought that he might drift off to the land
Of the dreaming, never awake and the angels would take his soul
Forever sleeping
He was very sad, for the one thing he had was his life
And he could not let go
He could not resist, for his eyes needed sleep
And to sleep is where he did go
As his eyes closed the angels arose
And to Heaven he went, I suppose.

**Casey Legg  (13)**
**Sir Joseph Williamson Mathematical School, Rochester**

*Young Writers - POP! Southern England*

# I Met At Dusk

I met at dusk the prince of night,
His cloak was made of twilight mists.
He swept a silent cat between the trees,
Hidden in a night-time moon.

He glided across the streams,
Whispering a thousand secrets of darkness.
To the naked eye, merely vapour.

He is clouds over country hills and fields.
As herds graze, he swoops a traveller,
Not noticing the silent intruder.

He returns a mere shadow to his home,
A dark, misty swamp.
He glides through the grasses to lie
And wait for dusk to come again.

I met at dusk the prince of night,
His cloak was made of twilight mists.
He swept a silent cat between the trees,
Hidden in a night-time moon.

**Thomas Selves (12)**
**Sir Joseph Williamson Mathematical School, Rochester**


# Responsible?

Passing greatness,
Do we ever see?
Believe we are too preoccupied by bleakness.
But when you see suffering, you gasp with grief.
Now don't be fake,
As if you care.
A few pennies, that is your responsibility.
Children mutilated - irrelevant.
As long as it is not ours.
Selfish people.
Will you change?
Well, we have not so far.

**Tola Adesina (17)**
**Sir Joseph Williamson Mathematical School, Rochester**

# Changes

My parents say I'm cheeky and I answer back these days
And that I'll be sent packing, if I don't mend my ways.
I must admit I rant and rave, I slam my door with zest,
The torture on my sister, is what I enjoy the best!

I see things differently now and make sure that I'm heard
And when I'm being told off, I don't listen to a word!
My parents think I'm lazy and want to throw away the key,
I tell them, blame my hormones, raging inside of me.

Sometimes when I go out, people stop and stare,
Is it my spots? My baggy pants? Or just my spiked-up hair?
I just stare back, pull a face and give them attitude,
Because I'm a teenager, they don't need to be so rude.

My voice has just gone husky, my nan thinks it's a cold,
She still thinks I'm seven, if the truth be told.
Has anyone noticed that I'm growing hairy, broad and tall?
Perhaps my little sister, who's definitely a 'know-it-all'!

My feet are getting bigger, my trousers are growing short,
I now pinch my dad's socks, but I've not yet been caught.
They say I gobble and rush my food, I wish they'd let me be,
They'll never understand, they've never been through puberty!

**Graeme Struthers  (14)**
**Sir Joseph Williamson Mathematical School, Rochester**


# The Fox

I lurk around in the night
And I give the chickens quite a fright.

I move quicker than a dart,
But yet I'm still very smart.

A hole in the ground,
Is what keeps me sound.

I've been hunted since birth
And soon, I'll just be within the earth.

**Ryan Evans  (13)**
**Sir Joseph Williamson Mathematical School, Rochester**

# Tiger, Tiger

I am a tiger,
I lurk in the tall, thin grass,
My stripes look like dead grass,
This helps me keep my stealth,
My rubbery paws beat onto the ground,
My fur has the softness of a new carpet.

In a split second I pounce,
Landing on the stray antelope,
I sink my sharp sword-like teeth in the neck of the animal,
It doesn't take long before the animal
Is nothing more than a dead carcass.

*But I can be cute!*

**Matthew Wren  (11)**
**Sir Joseph Williamson Mathematical School, Rochester**

# Eagle

The bird jumps out of its nest or lair,
Takes flight and swoops for food, it dares.
It glides around in a circular motion,
Through the skies as blue as an ocean.
Its large, sharp eyes survey the ground,
Its wings cut air without a sound.
It pinpoints its prey,
A rabbit at play.
It dives,
Through the sky
Aiming,
Killing.

**Jonathan Beck  (12)**
**Sir Joseph Williamson Mathematical School, Rochester**

# The Blaze

The smoke
Filtered in.
The door opened
I was greeted by a hallway full of the silent killer
Orange and red burned through the doors
Distant screams drowned by the burning blaze
Every room I knew oh so well, blurred as I rushed past them
Mixed with fiery colours
Down the stairs, dining room, kitchen. Where were they? My family
Freedom, the front door, my key to safety
Were they out there, calling for me?
Shouting out my name?
The seconds passed by
The fire gained power
Roaring
Destroying
Killing
Save myself!
Run!
I let my hand decide, I turned the handle
My feet fell onto the damp grass
Staring up
My life burning away
The tears burned as they rushed down my face
Heart torn
My life perished in the blaze
Sure, I was lucky to escape
But I had died long before I had even left the house
Sirens
Tears
Death.

**Tom Heath  (12)**
**Sir Joseph Williamson Mathematical School, Rochester**

# Mary And Her Little Dog

Mary had a little dog
It liked to lick her toes
And when she bent right to the floor
He licked and sucked her nose.

One summer's morning he got up
To find a lovely treat,
He jumped and ran right down the stairs
And found a pile of meat.

He licked and licked till all was gone
And now was in a mess,
The meat inside him made him sick,
All over Mary's dress.

Mary saw the dog and feared,
'What can I do?' she cried.
She phoned the number 999,
'Oh no, too late, he's died!'

Mary phoned the funeral man,
'He's dead and weighs a ton!'
The man was shocked like you and me,
'What has this woman done?'

He lay there not a sound or twitch,
'What have I done?' she said.
She put her head into her hands;
The dog rose from the dead!

**Harry Stevens  (13)**
**Sir Joseph Williamson Mathematical School, Rochester**

# The Predator And The Prey

One day I went out for a walk,
Along the riverside.
When I espied a little fish,
Who quickly tried to hide.

I chose a stick to prod him with,
Long and straight and brown.
I swished the water near to him,
But he swam quickly down.

I did not want to lose my prey,
So I walked into the river.
Again I tried to stab my friend,
When he began to shiver.

I was amazed to see this sight
And saw him slowly turn.
He stared at me with cold black eyes,
My heart began to burn.

A brightly-coloured fish appeared,
Which swam around my toes.
I slipped and fell into the mud
And smashed my precious nose.

The pretty fish swam up to me
And this is what she said,
'You tried to kill my dearest friend,
But hurt yourself instead.'

**Ben Elder  (13)**
**Sir Joseph Williamson Mathematical School, Rochester**

# Sailor Of The Open Sea

I am the sailor of the ocean blue,
I'm more intelligent than you.
I skim across the open waves,
But you capture us for your slaves.

You put us in your water shows,
We each have balls upon our nose,
We backflip, jump through burning hoops
And then you make us swim in loops.

You lock us up for viewing pleasure,
We don't get time for our leisure.
Why won't you humans just release us?
Unlock the cells, don't make a fuss.

We want to swim around the deep,
We only want to race and leap.
So humans, come undo your sins,
Come on, *release the dolphins.*

**Joe Evans (14)**
**Sir Joseph Williamson Mathematical School, Rochester**


# Happiness - Haiku

Warm glow inside you,
Jolt of joy inside your heart,
Skipping all about.

**Harshal Patel (11)**
**Sir Joseph Williamson Mathematical School, Rochester**

# Memories

The river that runs, oh so silently,
Bubbling over stones and rocks.
The willow that drapes itself over the stream
And the voices that flow in the wind.

It seems that the tree bark, old and wrinkly,
Tells of a time before the past,
A time no longer existing except as a memory,
In this enchanted wood.

How, one asks oneself, can this place be real?
Seemingly no life left here,
No creatures live here, but voices in the breeze,
Just nothingness full of something.

The something, however, is unable to see,
The something that so clearly is here,
The immensity of the surrounding feeling,
The something that was, no longer is.

It's just a memory.

**Tom Smith  (13)**
**Sir Joseph Williamson Mathematical School, Rochester**


# The Girl - Haiku

Thinking, wondering,
Hoping that she will come back,
Gazing at the text.

**Conor Laker  (11)**
**Sir Joseph Williamson Mathematical School, Rochester**

# Cheetah

I am a cheetah as fast as you think,
I will be gone before you even blink,
I'm yellow all over and also dotted,
This helps camouflage and not get spotted,
On all my feet there are deadly claws,
I have the power of these in my paws,
My advantage is my tremendous speed,
When I have caught my prey I make them bleed,
Every animal I see I'll give a shot,
I will use my body and what I've got,
Every animal that sees me will flee,
Making them run to an intolerable degree,
In the end I always win, never lose,
Losing to an animal is not an excuse.

**Thomas Mo  (13)**
**Sir Joseph Williamson Mathematical School, Rochester**

# The Winter Battle

The ice and snow lay all about,
Holding things in their icy grasp,
Turning the ground into a sheet of white.

The blood stains the perfect white snow,
The cold wind pierces the fighters' armour like a knife,
The fighters grow weak from the cold.

In the end, all is consumed by the cold,
The innocent lay dead all about, but their kings still sneer
At their dead men who fought so fiercely,
Mothers, fathers, brothers, sisters, friends,
Sit weeping for those they lost.

**Remy Holmes  (13)**
**Sir Joseph Williamson Mathematical School, Rochester**

# Sniper

Here I kneel, in the soaking wet mud
I look like a tree, I am consumed by my camouflage
No one can tell I am here, I am swallowed by the natural habitat
Do you want to play my game? It's a waiting game
No one knows what is coming to them, until they're told in the afterlife
I am like an invisible god
The god of death
But it's not all in my favour
If I get into trouble, I am the one who has to get out of it
There is no one to help me, I am on my own

There he is
There is the target
*He* is the target

I look through the sight
I put him in the middle of the cross,
Not the cross of God
But the cross of death

I breathe in the last breath before the shot
It is a horrible one, it jams your throat and makes you sweat
As I pull the trigger, I block out all feelings of emotion

There is a bang as the round is sent towards the target
The recoil goes through me like an earthquake
The target is struck, the mission is completed

I want to go, but I must become that tree once again
And disappear like I was never there.

**Paul Wilson (15)**
**Sir Joseph Williamson Mathematical School, Rochester**

# Deep Water

Moving along, quietly, softly moving
Down the old stone path,
She's there, just going, but . . . first she trips,
Then stumbles and falls,
Plummets like a stone, then *splash!*
That's it, adieu, farewell, she goes down and down and down,
Her sister nearby, staring down, grinning, smiling, watching.
No help comes,
She's trapped; she's lost in the dark, watery chasm,
She cannot get out; no one helps.

She cries out, 'Help me! I'll drown, I'll drown!'
The angry waters drown out the sound;
The water swallows her,
Suddenly, help comes at last!
The men and women nearby hear her cry for help,
They jump down into the deep, dismal pit,
Splashing in,
With rings and ropes,
They drag her out; she's dripping wet,
Just half her clothes.

The rest down there,
Her sister changes, a dark, glaring, grave look.
The poor girl nearly drowned that day; only one shoe came out.
The sister didn't seem too pleased,
I wonder why that was.
But did she really trip that day? (The sister wasn't pleased)
Did she stumble?
And did she, then, really trip
Before she took
The fall?

**Samuel Shackleton  (11)**
**Sir Joseph Williamson Mathematical School, Rochester**

# Auction Room

Noise is buzzing,
People bustling,
Lots of tables,
Lots of squabbling.

Many rich men,
Lots of screaming,
Very fusty,
Very smelly.

Auctioneers shouting,
Hands go flying,
Pictures hanging,
Money flashing.

Lots of china,
Plates and saucers,
Bowls and vases,
Toys and brooches.

Smooth surface,
Carpeted floor,
Lots of warm colours,
Many people sweating.

Busy day,
Ornaments go,
Crowds leave,
Suddenly . . . silence.

**Alex Daykin  (11)**
**Sir Joseph Williamson Mathematical School, Rochester**

# The Final Stop

The sound of the cruise
Selling lots of malt
And hearing the port
The many rustles
And lots of bustles
Sitting by the sea
And looking at the big oak tree
There are many people around
Hearing all different sounds
All those who look
See fishermen's hooks
Looking at the waves
Watching the distant haze
And having fun on the cruise.

**Lewis Moran (13)**
**Sir Joseph Williamson Mathematical School, Rochester**


# I Am A Hyena

I am a hyena so loud and mischievous;
I am a hyena so silly and funny;
I am a hyena so brave and strong;
I am a hyena so fast and determined.

I am the hyena who lives on the plains;
I am the hyena with those big black spots;
I am the hyena who has that strange rough hair;
I am the hyena that laughs all night.

I am a hyena with those long sharp fangs;
I am a hyena who hunts all day;
I am a hyena so active and delicate;
I am the hyena you fear all night.

**Harrison Land (11)**
**Sir Joseph Williamson Mathematical School, Rochester**

# Dis Place

I 'ate dis place
I ain't neva makin' mi bed
You say polish ya shoes
Some chance!
I don't see da money
'Bout ten quid would do me.

Ya want me to eat mi veggies
Don't be silly
They're mank
I wanna go out
No, you say, too bad, ya grounded
Good luck, bye!

I come 'ome and play the PlayStation
You say do ya 'omework
I ain't got none
He starts givin' me evils
I say to him don't give me evils
You get me in a stress!

**Connor Ashenden (13)**
**Sir Joseph Williamson Mathematical School, Rochester**

# Dragon

I am a dragon,
I destroy lives.
Every day I burn villages
And feast off men's wives.

Nothing will last,
That stands in my path.
Until one brave soul comes one day,
To save me from eternal life . . .

At last.

**Thomas Lloyd (11)**
**Sir Joseph Williamson Mathematical School, Rochester**

# Waking Up To Snow

Snowflakes falling all around,
Gently floating to the ground.
A gentle layer of soft white,
About three inches fell last night.

A light crisp blanket lay around,
Not a noise, not a sound.
No one moving in the street,
Just a track from someone's feet.

Here comes the postman through the gate,
I think the snow has made him late.
Wrapped up warm, can't see his face,
Walking like they do in space.

There's no school, the teacher's stuck,
Isn't that a bit of luck!
Let's get dressed and off we go!
To spend our day out in the snow!

**Kierran Boden (12)**
**Sir Joseph Williamson Mathematical School, Rochester**

# Zoo

The hustle and bustle of people pushing through;
A huge crowd of tourists obstructing the view.

Elephants are eating and consuming with greed;
Monkeys, howling and hooting for food, do they plead?

Zookeepers are sweeping the mud-covered ground;
Tour guides are showing what in the jungles they found.

The gift shop is full of many souvenirs;
There are books, plastic elephants, snakes and bears.

**Julian McManus (12)**
**Sir Joseph Williamson Mathematical School, Rochester**

# The Perfect Hunter

At hunting prey, I have a gift,
I'm powerfully built, fast and swift.
I've a fierce manner and a deep growl,
Up to the moon I often howl.

I've grey-white fur and a pointy nose,
A bushy tail and claws on my toes.
Very sharp teeth and yellow eyes
And small white ears that point to the skies.

Many fear me and rightly so,
I'm a ruthless hunter on soil and snow.
I'm hunting a pack with my fellow kin,
We've seen the prey and we're moving in.

The deer are standing on a large, snowy hill,
We need the meat, so have to kill.
We choose our prey, an injured male,
We start to run, we will not fail.

A head turns, they start to flee,
Our target can't run, he has a damaged knee.
We catch him soon, we can sense his fear;
Then we attack and the end is near.

**Tom Seed  (13)**
**Sir Joseph Williamson Mathematical School, Rochester**

# A Place - Haiku

I found an alley
This is my little secret
The place where I stand.

**Zeshan Mirza  (11)**
**Sir Joseph Williamson Mathematical School, Rochester**

# Europe 1915

The constant stink of death
Wanders, almost visible, above the carnage.
Seeking out the living, the dying
The old, the young.

Pits of mud house the men;
Barren land separates them.
Covered in unburied corpses;
The dead spared no dignity.

Somewhere a whistle screams
Followed by a terrible cry;
A cry mixed with fear, with anger
A cry to keep out the dread.

And as the grey uniforms rise
So do the rifles of the green
And then the bark of machine guns,
Mow down more men.

So many men
Fall onto that barren land.
The land carved and pounded by artillery;
To look like the surface of the moon.

**Talos Tsavellas  (13)**
**Sir Joseph Williamson Mathematical School, Rochester**


# Guitar

Guitar, notes, practise, strum,
Amplifier, plectrum, play,
Gig, money, proud Mum,
Great, girlfriend, *stay!*

**Phillip Vidler  (12)**
**Sir Joseph Williamson Mathematical School, Rochester**

# The Rhino

I charge when I'm angry,
Women only see me once a year,
I may be large, but I'm fast and strong,
If you make me angry, you'll regret it.

I live in Africa in the sun,
My cousins are white,
Even though they're black,
I'm endangered, hunted by bullies.

My horn is like a white thorn sticking out of my nose,
My skin is rough and grey,
Although my sight is bad,
My hearing is great.

Who am I?
Go on, guess . . .
I'm a rhino!

**Lewis Bailey (11)**
**Sir Joseph Williamson Mathematical School, Rochester**


## Down At The Supermarket

Golden honey, freezing milk,
Tie-dyed clothes made out of silk,
Fruity juices, golden fries,
Stinky onions make you cry.
Glowing light bulbs, fizzy coke,
Fags for people that like to smoke,
Jelly Tots in the sweetie aisle,
Classy chocolates make you smile,
Smelly flowers, perfect things,
Someone might buy you a ring.

**Aaron Dimmick (14)**
**Sir Joseph Williamson Mathematical School, Rochester**

# Daredevil

Nervously, I sit waiting for the signal,
Red, amber, green,
I pull the trigger and off I go.

Rolling forwards, faster and faster,
The moment of truth is soon to become,
As the sun appears, I shall conquer my fear.

As the speed increases,
I fly off the ramp,
There's no going back.

The ground draws closer,
Faster and faster.

The wheels hit the tarmac,
The screech of brakes,
Heard all around.

The crowd go wild as I accept the golden medal,
My team are smiling, happy that I won,
Now is the end of a brilliant day as I ride away.

**Ryan Dennis (11)**
**Sir Joseph Williamson Mathematical School, Rochester**


# War Of The Poppies

Bodies Fall,
Smoke so tall,
Best friend dead,
Bullet in his head,
Nobody survives,
No one alive,
Disease is writhe.

Everyone knows,
Trench foot is here,
Killing those who are left,
The ones who survive there are none,
The war of the poppies cannot be won.

**Alex Mortley (12)**
**Sir Joseph Williamson Mathematical School, Rochester**

# Bats Of The Dark

Born of darkness,
yet creature of air.
Bat by my name
and fangs I do bear.

Shunned by others,
for living without sun.
While they're in the light,
in the dark I do run.

Soft fur is framed,
by leather wing.
Writhing in unearthly silence,
how I sing, how I sing.

By the night I hunt you,
by my own decree.
By the night I hunt you,
by the night I see.

My ruby eyes do spy you,
lying deep in sleep.
My body quivers in earnest,
for the flesh I will soon reap.

But still you're not afraid of me,
my size dispels your fear.
But you will be scared of me,
I assure you, when I'm near.

**Liam Dooley (11)**
**Sir Joseph Williamson Mathematical School, Rochester**

# The Swimming Pool

Teenagers diving
And parents striving,
To get their kids under control,
In the swimming pool.

Babies crying,
People are drying,
The lifeguard's diving in and out,
Of the swimming pool.

Children splashing,
Bathers clashing,
People getting out to have lunch,
In the swimming pool.

Fresh smell of chips,
Boys doing flips,
The lifeguard telling them not to,
In the swimming pool.

A mother near the water,
Screaming at her daughter,
The tears streaming down her face,
In the swimming pool.

Hustle and bustle,
In the swimming pool,
Dropping and diving,
In the swimming pool.

The most busy, bustling, brimming place in town,
The swimming pool, it is.

**Sam Heyes (11)**
**Sir Joseph Williamson Mathematical School, Rochester**

# The Busiest Place In The World

It is a Friday night;
There is barely any light
I've just finished school
As I enter the hall,
Mum comes to greet me
While I put away the key;
This is the busiest place in the world I can see.

As I go upstairs
My baby sisters are acting like they're teddy bears,
My other sister is writing about her latest crush,
While my brother shaves his moustache;
My scientific dad is growing the smallest ever tree
When Mum calls for tea,
This is the busiest place in the world I can see.

There's a scramble throughout the place,
Even with the little dormouse,
Everyone jumps to their chairs
While I'm still walking down the stairs,
When will this curse set me free?
I don't think this will ever be,
This is the busiest place in the world I can see.

After dinner brother sets off for his job,
While I write about this hectic mob
My eldest sister
Sprays some smelly stuff on her blister,
It's time for bed
Now that everyone has been fed
This is the busiest place in the world I can see.

**Jack Johnston  (11)**
**Sir Joseph Williamson Mathematical School, Rochester**

# Fleance Speaks . . .

*(Inspired by Macbeth)*

A letter from Fleance (shortly after his father's death) explaining
How his father Banquo, was really murdered . . .

To thee I beg you flee today,
For thou safety and mine is clear to pay,
That wretched Macbeth, who had created a shudder,
Demoted his friends and brewed up this thunder.

Clouds that are looming,
Shading our light,
Builds tension and murder, no doubt creating a fight,
Letter of sorrows, letter of grief,
Praise be to Banquo, his life far too brief.

What purpose you ask? One searches their mind,
Why it's the truth of the matter; I shalt no be kind.
Treacherous Macbeth, no mercy had he,
Three murtherers were sent to slay father and me,
Villainous; cruel; malevolent; immoral,
Expedition of woodland ended in incurable quarrel.

Banquo, he was brave, put up a valiant fight,
Unable to succeed by the three murtherers might.
'Flee, Fleance, flee!'
My father did say,
Forgetting those words would perhaps keep my mind at bay.

But to express my thoughts now is a weight off my chest,
My maturity strengthened with my dad laid to rest.
His death was a mourning that hath altered my being,
Which links back to the warning in urgency of fleeing.

Thou who you callest King, shalt be King no more;
Dead also shalt be that queenly whore!

**Lawrence Clemence (15)**
**Sir Joseph Williamson Mathematical School, Rochester**

# Cannon

A figure of beauty and death,
Rolling into battle like a beetle.
Finds its target, a quivering enemy,
Pack in the gunpowder, then the cartridge, then the cannonball.
The fuse is lit, sparks fly then,
The sound of the cannon and the screams of men
Flying backwards fells the ear,
The smell of burnt powder and blood fills the nose.
Death is upon them,
They turn to flee, but it is too late for them,
Another cannonball flies into an unlucky few backs,
The sound of crunching bone is also heard.

The next enemy target appears in the city,
The titanic cathedral pokes out of the city and dominates
All other buildings,
The perfect target.
Ten balls fly at it at once, as the commander barks orders
To the rest of the men,
The tower crumbles revealing the massive bells.
They come to the ground unleashing a deafening clang,
For the enemy it seems as if Armageddon is upon them,
The rest of the cathedral collapses under the strain
Crushing a few houses too.
The day is done,
The war is won.
The enemy is on its knees,
Their empire crushed,
Their city's burnt like a child with a magnifying glass playing with ants
The day is done,
The war is won.

**George Anderson  (12)**
**Sir Joseph Williamson Mathematical School, Rochester**

# Rebel!

You say dat I'm trouble,
Now dat just ain't fair!
Ya say I'm a problem,
Does it look like I care?
Ya say, 'Speak words proper,'
Like I speak like a chav!
Ya ask, do I take drugs?
Does it look like I 'ave?
Ya shout at me lots,
When I spill stuff on da floor.
Ya tell me to get out,
On my way I'll shut da door!
Ya speak like I'm a baby,
Don' tell wot a do.
I'll make my own decision, fanks,
I've already made a few!
I fought of what to do at school,
I rebelled against the head.
They had to take him home to rest,
I egged him in his bed!
They called me in to 'ave a go,
Suspend me, dey said dey would.
I said to dem I did not care,
I suppose I really should.
So now I wanna fight,
I wanna smack 'em in da face!
'Cause I ain't a school kid anymore,
I'm a rebel in a race!
Dere ain't no one like me,
Not a chav in all da world,
Who rebels around like I do,
I'm going to be heard!

**Lee Bell  (13)**
**Sir Joseph Williamson Mathematical School, Rochester**

# All We Need

All we need is . . .
Food in our bellies,
Hats on our heads,
Water to quench us,
Sheets on our beds.

All we need is . . .
Teachers to teach us,
Shoes on our feet,
Trousers and T-shirts,
Shelter and heat.

All we need is . . .
Someone to help us,
Someone to love,
Hope for the future,
Light from above,
Because I live in the Third World.

**Billy Allen (12)**
**Sir Joseph Williamson Mathematical School, Rochester**


# The Rhino

In the distance of the African plains,
You see a big beefy rhino drinking its water in all its pride,
He stands up all relaxed and strong,
You come closer you see his frail, grey skin.

He feels hungry, the rhino starts to run to his food,
As the Earth shakes the animals in the plain run away,
As the rhino approaches his lovely lush grass,
The grass is shaking like a tree in the wind.

As the rhino scoffs his grass,
He starts to feel tired,
He rushes back to his watering hole,
When he lies down he knows he will not wake up till early afernoon.

**Sebastian Mouzo (11)**
**Sir Joseph Williamson Mathematical School, Rochester**

# The Airport

Wheels squeaking
Drinks leaking
Children screaming
Adults speaking

People depart
Attendants look smart
Captains take charge
Passengers letharge

Junk food is bad
Nothing else to be had
We eat 'cause we're bored
And 'cause we can't yet board

Flights are delayed
Nerves are frayed
Tempers high
Babies cry

On the plane at last
But times goes not fast
Squashed in our seats
Hurry! Get us there, please!

**James Chittil  (14)**
**Sir Joseph Williamson Mathematical School, Rochester**

# I Ain't Done Nuttin

Yo Muva,
You keep hittin' me but not ma bruva,
Why you doin dis to me?
You always fink I'm naughty.
Is it cos I always be tellin' porkys,
Weneva I'm playin' on ma phone,
You never let me buy a ringtone,
'N' Father,
You ain't much different r ya,
You always shout at me,
Ma sister dus some tings bad, don't she?
Dis is well out of order,
Now you're goin' well over da border,
It's now time for me to leave 'ome,
'N' I won't forget ma garden gnome,
See ya, wouldn't wanna be ya!

**Adil Yaqub (12)**
**Sir Joseph Williamson Mathematical School, Rochester**


# Dis Really Isn't Fair

Yo Nan! I is writing to complain,
About de homework,
Dat you is settin' me,
It is jus' so not fair.

De uniform me look,
like a fool,
And we'd all like to look proper cool,
Dey all jus' laugh at us when we is in school.

Dis jus' really ain't fair,
Dat no one even care,
Dey jus' make me sit on the floor,
And makes us pay more!

Init Bruv!

**George Whiley (12)**
**Sir Joseph Williamson Mathematical School, Rochester**

# The Red Spitting Cobra

I sleep through day*sss*,
And hunts as night*sss*,
I'm medium-sized to all my friends,
But beware the sight of my red scaly skin.

I can spit from my mouth to poison you,
But if you're lucky enough I might just mi*ss*,
If not you'll be lying on the floor;
That's when the fun will begin.

If you live in Egypt then beware,
Because I might just come and attack you;
So beware my approach or you'll never make it,
If you want to live then keep away and leave me alone.

So now you've heard what I am like,
And know where I live,
Then you shall know my name,
If not then quiver with fear.

**Karun Singh (12)**
**Sir Joseph Williamson Mathematical School, Rochester**


# Car Crash

Burnt cars crumbling,
Pedestrian mumbling,
As the flames start to die,
The babies start to cry.

As the children hold hands,
The coppers put up the security bands,
As the police officers investigate,
The firemen are already late.

**Richard Taylor (11)**
**Sir Joseph Williamson Mathematical School, Rochester**

# Reading Festival

At Reading Festival,
People are sweaty and hot,
Crowd-surfing is banned
But actually it happens a lot.

As the music starts,
The crowd will start to cheer,
They sing along to their favourite songs,
Then they wander off to buy a beer.

Some acts are loved, others hated,
Some acts adored, others berated.
Flags are waved, bottles are thrown,
Some the most famous bands in the world, others unknown.

At the end of the weekend,
People emerge from their tents.
They have their last beer
And wait for next year.

**Cameron Bishop  (12)**
**Sir Joseph Williamson Mathematical School, Rochester**

# Chathamese Protest

Yo Mum, I'm now thirteen,
On cleaning my bedroom, you know I ain't too keen!
Mum you're way sad,
After all, my bedroom ain't even that bad.
You chucked all my stuff away that had my books init,
And den u tell me u ain't seen it,
Why should I 'ave to do all dis stuff for you?
You could at least get me sum tn's and a pair of shoes.
You tell me to clean the TV quick,
But I jus' feel like givin' it a kick.
You always make me hoover da floor,
Even worse you make me suck on an apple core.
My bruv don't ever get to do his work,
When he looks, he gives me a smile,
You know I like singing all of da time,
So please don't make a shut up sign!

**Sunil Landa  (12)**
**Sir Joseph Williamson Mathematical School, Rochester**

# Wimbledon

The best two weeks of the year are here,
Today!
Who will watch and who will play,
All you hear is lots of kids shouting!
Or you could watch some pretty flowers sprouting,
Even in the darkest days people will come to watch and
Praise.

Then you've got the people shopping,
Always, chatting, never stopping,
Gathering around Centre Court,
People are watching as they were taught!
Then the ball goes pip, pap, pop!

Then there is a sudden stop . . .
Then it starts to
Rain!
And what a great shame.

But then the sun finds a gap,
Then comes a roar and a great big clap,
Then people start chomping on strawberries,
Plus iced buns topped with cherries,
Then the day comes to an end.

I wonder what will happen tomorrow . . .

**Jack Hicklin (11)**
**Sir Joseph Williamson Mathematical School, Rochester**

# Strike!

Yo Sir,
I fink dat dis school is rubbish,
Firstly,
Right,
You mek's pick up de litta,
Den we get bitta,
So you go mad,
And we call you sad,
All da teachers fink dat dey are betta dan us,
But dey ain't nuffin compared to us,
You don't let us use our phones in school,
'Cause you reckon dat dey distract us,
Why do we 'ave to do all dis 'riting,
When we don't learn anyfink from it?
All da teachers go on about da 'free Rs',
But even I know dat, riting don't 'ave a 'r' at de start,
But,
Right,
Worst of all you mek's wear dis 'orrible outfit widda tie,
You make us do our top buttons up,
So we suffocate,
Even da teachers don't 'ave to wear smart clodes,
'Cause I saw de PE teacher,
Wearing tracky bottoms,
I say strike, if da school don't change.

**Ben Dance (12)**
**Sir Joseph Williamson Mathematical School, Rochester**

# Complaint

Why do I 'ave to clean mi room Mum?
It ain't even dirtee,
Come on please,
Why do I 'ave to,
I ain't made no mess,
It was mi mates,
De threw mi clothes on da floor,
Not mi!
I ain't broke mi bed dat was mi bro CJ,
Don't blame 'im do ya?
And I didn't do nutink to da TV,
It was like dat when I came in.

Stop pressurin' mi Mum,
I ain't a kid no more,
I will do mi 'omework,
But later, and anyway da footy is on, it is Charlton Vs Chelsea,
At da Valley,
Come on Mum, Charlton 'ave a great chance of winnin',
And I don't want to miss it.

Alright Mum you win, I will tidy mi room,
. . . And do mi 'omework,
But in future don't pressure mi again.

**Daniel Forster (12)**
**Sir Joseph Williamson Mathematical School, Rochester**

# The Betrayed Servant

I carry you people all through the day.
Taking none of your money or pay.
The saddle itches, never growing lighter,
But I struggle through because I am a fighter.

Riding round the paddock all of the day,
All for a measly bundle of hay.
The tiresome rope is always gnawing,
The endless routine is ever so boring.

The work would be hard if not for my bed,
I'm pleased with my keeper, all rosy and red.
But my owner is the only good human round here,
That is something that is perfectly clear.

Every other human that comes near me,
Will never ever let me be.
For no reason at all I'm punched and kicked,
And they laugh as I flinch when my ears are flicked.

One day I decide *no more, no more!*
And I kick one of them away to the floor.
The others try to pull me away,
But I am not so easily kept at bay.

I break free, and trample the rest,
This will show them that I am the best.
I am away, running and flying,
Almost free, *bang;* dying.

**Jack Neil (13)**
**Sir Joseph Williamson Mathematical School, Rochester**

# Believe Me

At school dey are scary,
Especially the teacha called Mary.
She whips ya wid de cane if ya is bad,
Sometimes if ya a good lad!
Den dey sen ya ta da corna,
An be rude 'bait ya.
Dey is always nasty, an' a bit feisty,
I would give dem a piece of mi mind,
If I weren't bind ta da rules.
I 'ate dem all, but dey carry on an' bawl,
I wish dey would go away.
Wid o' widout der pay.
Eva dat o' da floor swallows me 'ole,
An I would go,
Ya do believe me Mum,
I'm not lyin' coz I'm dumb,
I do solemnly swear dat it is truth,
But I know dat you'll say it ain't da truth.

**Daniel Cruse (12)**
**Sir Joseph Williamson Mathematical School, Rochester**

# The Raindrop's Ride

Flowing sickly quickly,
Ever so slickly.

On a hot day,
Flying away.

Transparent and blue,
Not much to do.

From the herd of darkness,
A drop of starkness.

Falling through the air so cold,
A raindrop never been bold.

On to a umbrella,
Into the mouth of 'yonder fella',

The ecosystem of the Earth,
Born in a watery birth.

**Nathan Wilkins  (13)**
**Sir Joseph Williamson Mathematical School, Rochester**

# I 'Ate It

Why do ya treat mi like dis?
Always tellin' mi to go to bed,
And tidyin' mi room,
I 'ate it.

I 'ate da way you always tell us off,
And I 'ate da way you take mi sweets away,
You never let mi go out by miself,
I 'ate it.

You never let mi go on a school trip,
You always hav' to spoil everyfin',
You always look a mi texts,
I 'ate it.

You always read mi emails,
You will tell mi off if I break somefin,
Or get paint on da table,
I 'ate it.

You take all mi toys away,
And mi games,
You won't even let mi watch TV,
I 'ate it.

**Jason Degiorgio  (12)**
**Sir Joseph Williamson Mathematical School, Rochester**

# The Subway

I wake up; it's that day today,
Time to use the US subway.
In the air I smell espresso,
But don't spill it on your pants or you'll be in a messo!
In the rush hour I push hurriedly,
Trying to get on the subway rather worriedly.
Outside the subway door there's a cop,
Even outside the bagel shop.
Outside the toilets teenagers are kissing,
Although I'm desperate I'll give it a missing.
On the train it's packed real tight,
You can't get a seat without a fight.
Sipping my espresso I'm not too sure,
Did I put in two sugars or perhaps many more?
The lovely smell wafting up my nose,
*Blast* I just spilt some on my clothes,
So now I must get off the train,
Knowing tomorrow I must go again.

**Yousef Khan (12)**
**Sir Joseph Williamson Mathematical School, Rochester**

# The Train

The chuffing train
steams along
the rusty,
rippled
track.
It's
black
beauty
running
rampant
without
a care of danger. Creating a breeze that makes even the
trees hang loosely, little bugs sway in the wind out of control.
It's like a snake slithering along a bamboo ready to strike with
utter precision wherever it goes. The wheels creak like a star
falling            out            of            place.

o        o        o        o        o

The tracks chatter to each other like parrots gone mad.

**Michael Fegan  (11)**
**Sir Joseph Williamson Mathematical School, Rochester**

# The Grand Piano

Inside
My diaphragm
My silky sinews are
Being s t r e t c h e d.
I am very sharp at spotting flats.
When I play peacefully ever so often, my heartbeat
Increases. I can play *piano* or *forte.* My speech that echoes
From my diaphragm sounds high and practised. My body is
A polished surface, from which intricate shapes are eminent.
My voice can be heard across the hall, as I sing out. I have
85 black and white keys, yet none of them open my little
Luminous lock. Below my little lock I have two feet
Which pedal paternalistically along with my music. Nice and
Gently they hop      to      the      beat. Funny though
How I have three                    legs and two feet
But I can't                    seem to walk!

**Ashley Mergulhao (12)**
**Sir Joseph Williamson Mathematical School, Rochester**

# Signs

As I travel down this dark, distorted road of disbelief,
I pass sign after sign like a never-ending circle of grief.
Many different options confuse my fragile mind,
As the jagged edges of the concrete,
Pierce the tender flesh of my feet,
Causing a river of blood,
That stains the coarse, grey, grave ground,
And leaves me tormented . . .

Until I spot that one unique sign which catches my eye,
My mind is suddenly fuelled with a strange sense of anticipation,
And the path to which it leads me is short, but how it does
                                              inspire me,
A multitude of reds, oranges, pinks and purples lie upon the
                                              horizon,
Enriching its perfect scenery of soft, lush, green grass,
And pools of cool, clear water, which soothe my travelling wounds,
The sweet scent of pollen lingers in the crisp, clean air,
Forcing my lungs to leap from within me.

But it does not last long, for the path ends suddenly,
And the sunset which presented itself to me,
Gently fades away behind a dazzling dark cloud,
That paints an image of black and grey,
Swirling together upon a bright white canvass,
The sun displays its every detailed shadow,
As its thunderous roar enhances that bright blue blade,
Spectacular to observe, though deadly to incur.

I know I am back on this path of pain,
As my feet harden once more to endure its harsh terrain,
And my pupils expand to capture each small prism of light,
That breaks through the clouds,
With a sense of destination to show the route to carry on,
Along this never-ending circle of grief,
Until another sign appears.

**Richard Smale (17)**
**Sir Joseph Williamson Mathematical School, Rochester**

# The Man Across The Road

It was a cold morning,
Everything seemed to have an unusually brittle texture.
I was still yawning, just out of a nice warm bed,
A cold wind slashed my ears,
And I saw him.
He walked like he could take on anything,
Like a power followed him,
Like time revered him.
He strutted past a shop,
As if he never wanted to stop,
While some raindrops hit my coat.

His hat at an awkward angle,
His hunched shape radiating a cold secrecy.
In the distance a driver did struggle with a steering wheel
                                         out of control.
On the other side of the road,
The man's coat covered the width of the pavement.
That khaki great coat looked a heavy load,
With its tips brushing the ground.
Then the car was close, gaining speed:
It swerved and turned towards the man.
With an almighty crash,
The window behind opened with a smash.

There was no enquiry.
No body was found.
In the end, it seems,
There was no man around.
No bones were broken,
No scream was heard,
No corpse lay still,
As the engine burned.

**John Sharpe  (14)**
**Sir Joseph Williamson Mathematical School, Rochester**

# The King Is Dead

What is done is done they say,
But death - that never goes away,
It's always there, just out of sight,
A kingdom reeking of a grisly plight,
For when you're dead Death rings a bell,
And sends you down, right down to Hell,
A desolate, rocky, ruined land,
Reflecting treasures you've never found,
And there directly opposite,
A burning, churning, fiery pit!
With screaming skeletons burning well,
Enchanted by a magic spell!
Forcing them to feel again,
Excruciating, dying pain,
Sticks and swords and spears and stones,
Disease devouring their bones,
And there - slashing them clean apart,
Are maggots eating through their hearts,
And then a booming voice they hear,
That freezes dead each dying ear,
A sudden flash then soon occurs,
Which makes their long gone vision blur,
And then - the King of Dead they see!
Who soon will be the king of ye!
They stare straight at him, frozen in fear,
And cry, 'Our Lord the Devil's here!'

**William Friend (12)**
**Sir Joseph Williamson Mathematical School, Rochester**

# Mi Life

I always duz mi bedroom,
I is needin' a big break,
I always in doom 'n' gloom,
Cleanin' mi room makes me shake.

Mi mum likes ta shout out,
In mega 'igh tones,
'Get up yu lazi lout,'
It puts chills in mi bones.

I'm wantin' dis to stop,
She's getting on my wick,
The smell of this mop,
Is making me feel sick.

She gives me a duster,
Then flicks it in mi face,
''Urry up Busta,
You're getting in mi face.'

I ain't goin' to clean mi room,
That's mi muvver's job,
It's 'er dustpan and broom,
I'll jus' give 'er sum gob!

I luv 'er really,
She's mi mum,
I don't express myself clearly,
I'm just a bit dum!

**James Shiel (12)**
**Sir Joseph Williamson Mathematical School, Rochester**

# Init

I jus' wannid ter say,
Dat school is rubbish, init?
Wot da we akshally do,
Dat'z any use?
Nuffin.
You teachers fink yer so smart,
Wiv all yer spellings an' dat.
Bu' ter be honest, we jus' don't
Givva stuff.
Do we?
Inglish is jus' a load ov
Rubbish, wiv verbs an' nans an' stuff.
And maffs, well s'jus' a load ov
Crappy numbers.
Init?
Wot's da deal wid dis 'omework?
Wot's da poin if we go school?
We migh' as well not do it,
Dis 'omework.
I' stupid.
All youz teachers are well stressy,
Yer jus' moan, moan, moan, moan, moan.
So wot if sumwun ain't da
Brightes' bulb?
School's rubbish, init?

**Tom Warway  (13)**
**Sir Joseph Williamson Mathematical School, Rochester**

# Monitor Lizard

I'm the king of the lizards,
Greatest of them all.
They are scared of me,
Because I'm powerful.

I move fast,
At quite a speed.
I'm solitary,
I need no lead.

I keep myself a secret,
Though I'm not shy.
Even though I'm hiding,
I'm awfully sly.

I stalk my prey,
My weekly meal.
Once I've eaten,
How good I feel.

I live in my burrow,
And guard it well.
I'll detect an intruder,
With my great sense of smell.

I'm quite large,
But very stealthy.
I can catch my victim,
Even if it's healthy.

**Louis Wheeler (12)**
**Sir Joseph Williamson Mathematical School, Rochester**

# My Life As A Cricket

I'm sorry if I scared you,
I only wanted to say hello;
I jumped up and kissed you,
But you flicked me away.

The stag beetle and grasshoppers,
They're the evil ones;
They jump and scuttle after me,
But they don't only want to say hello.

Then you trap me in a jam jar,
And stare at me night and day;
At least I'm closer to you,
But there's nowhere to lay!

I weep and yelp,
And cry for help;
You don't even stop and stare,
I don't want to scare.

I hate being a cricket,
Nobody gives a care;
I might as well not live,
Life really isn't fair!

**Sam Cornell  (12)**
**Sir Joseph Williamson Mathematical School, Rochester**

# A Day At The Cinema

You can see the children jumping,
You can see the children bumping,
You can see the children thumping,
Or they're dumping their stuff on the floor.

You can hear the girls screaming,
And the dads dreaming that they had a new son or daughter,
You can hear the mums and dads speaking,
And the door creaking.

The smell of popcorn makes mouths water,
While funny cartoons bring lots of laughter,
As the children are lacking discipline,
You can hear the movie starting.

And the line is finally moving,
The kids are screaming in delight,
And the dads are covered in fright,
At last they are in and it's quiet.

**Samuel Perkins  (12)**
**Sir Joseph Williamson Mathematical School, Rochester**

# Budget Fairy Tale

Open up to a new world,
Where things aren't what they seem.
People aren't what they say,
And all the signs lead the wrong way.
Welcome to this place,
Where the world falls at your feet.
Only to bring you down with it,
There is no one to hold on to.
No one listens or will understand,
You look for someone to be your rock,
No one will be here to hold your hand.
Welcome to your own mind,
Where you shut yourself off from reality.
You wish that there is a way out,
You think that there has to be.
Welcome to your personal Hell,
No one cares to bid you well.
You took all that people had,
And cried and cried as if you were sad.
Begging for forgiveness,
Give the master his comeuppance,
But once again you failed him.
It's your budget fairy tale,
You have everything you want,
But when it comes down to it,
Everything goes wrong for you,
It's your budget fairy tale.
All you have now is a shard,
It was because of your disregard.

**Alex Souter  (15)**
**Sir Joseph Williamson Mathematical School, Rochester**

# All In The Red And White Tent

Outside the tent,
It is hailing, small kids wailing,
Tills chiming, children whining,
Burgers frying, people buying,
Tickets fluttering, adults muttering,
'Hooray! Into the tent!'

Clowns tooting, kids hooting,
Acrobats flying, babies crying,
Announcers announcing, lions pouncing,
Strong men lifting, merchants drifting,
Seals flipping, doughnuts dipping,
Sawdust stinking, old men blinking,
Popcorn popping, ice cream slopping,
Applause! The show's over!

Outside the tent,
Cleaners brushing, people rushing,
Lions sleeping, babies weeping,
Vans starting, people parting,
*Brrrm!* Off into the distance,
To travel the world.

**Tom Unthank  (11)**
**Sir Joseph Williamson Mathematical School, Rochester**

# 'Omework

'Omework is so borin' and dull,
I mean, who'd wanna spend their 'ole time,
Doin 'omework?
I dunno why the schools 'ave t' set so much,
They 'ardly give you any time t' do it anyway,
Parents is just as bad, 'Do this, do that, write that, change this!'
I don't fink so!

Some of the subjects we has t' do,
Take too long, 'istory essays, geography projects, German
words an' all,
The fing I 'ate the most is art,
All you ever do is sit there,
Listen t' the teacher drone on 'bout differen' artists an' pictures.

I'd be a lot 'appier stayin' at 'ome,
Playin' on me games console or playin' footy in the park,
Ban 'omework, that's wha' I say.

**Jack Paulley  (12)**
**Sir Joseph Williamson Mathematical School, Rochester**

# The Bear

I'm furry and strong,
When I stretch out I look long.

I pounce if I'm annoyed,
Out from under the trees.

I like hunting with my claws,
And don't like to share space.

My long brown fur is rustling about,
If you anger me I start to howl.

When I stroll around the deep forest,
I walk around relaxed.

I am patient when I hunt at the lake,
Waiting for the perfect fish.

By now you should know,
That I am the bear.

**Andrew Poile  (11)**
**Sir Joseph Williamson Mathematical School, Rochester**

# London

Big Ben is booming,
Bells are clanging,
People are shouting,
Cameras are flashing.
Men are running,
Cars are speeding,
Dogs are barking,
Babies are screaming,
Boys are dreaming.
Bus drivers are horning;
They say, 'Get up it's the morning,'
Children are moaning,
Teachers are phoning,
Mechanics are fixing,
I can smell burgers,
Or are they murders?
People eating fish and chips,
And then they hear a crash,
And people say, 'Quick let's dash.'

**Hiran Ram  (12)**
**Sir Joseph Williamson Mathematical School, Rochester**

# I Am A Dolphin

I swim through the sea,
So fast and free.
I am a kind of creature,
I will not attack you unless you attack me.

I am fun to play with,
Always excited.
Loved by children,
Cherished by swimmers.

But I am also the cleverest animal in the sea,
I can outwit sharks,
And be as cunning as a fox.

My eyes are full of wonder and curiosity,
My skin as smooth as a new boiled egg.

And if one day you are lucky enough,
You might even hear,
My squeaky little melody.

I am a dolphin!

**Aaron Thompson  (11)**
**Sir Joseph Williamson Mathematical School, Rochester**

# Goldfish

The window we can see,
But we are not free;
The door we can see,
But we are not free.

Our golden bodies shine,
But we cannot find
The way out of this cell;
You could say we are in Hell.

We get fed dried bread;
We don't even have a bed,
We fish need rights!
We should stand up and fight!

We can't stand up and fight,
Even with all our might;
We need water to breathe,
And we cannot leave.

**Andre White (13)**
**Sir Joseph Williamson Mathematical School, Rochester**

# The Lighthouse

You
*shine bright and boldly,* tell us
*danger is near and to keep* away.
Three men
keeping
themselves
amused inside
a candy stick
waiting for supplies
and food. The vast
ocean shimmering in
the moonlight with danger
never far away. Sometimes
the angry sea will lash you, but
you stand steadfast as you
have done for the last hundred years.
Many sailors have you to thank for
saving them from a watery grave.
Long may your light shine and the
steady rocks hold you firm and still.

**Alex Williams (11)**
**Sir Joseph Williamson Mathematical School, Rochester**

# A Cursed Love

A winged plea,
A songman's noose,
A dead girl's wish.
Love, the curse.

Beauty pageant in their spring best,
A stuttering boy in black,
A warm hand held in the dark.
Love steals all this away.

Cupid gives us dreams,
Venus gave us stars,
God gave us hearts.
Love took them all.

Eyes to see your lover,
Arms to hold their heart,
Feet to swing them round the floor.
Love makes them disappear.

Souls of gold that glitter,
Feelings that float on air,
Charms that make you sink to your knees.
Love is their antidote.

A desired wedding,
A newborn child,
The first kiss in the dark.
Love is the curse.

Of all our souls,
For a waltz of treachery,
Is still for the insightful,
Than all of man's works.
To accursed love.

**Katherine Baker  (15)**
**The Atherley School, Southampton**

# Thunderstorm

Crunching and crashing,
As it crawls over the trees into the town,
People gallop away in terror.

Rain slapping on the roofs of quivering houses,
And the rattle of the wind on the windows,
Is like a rattlesnake's tail shaking in fear.

A flash of light,
Like a candle being blown out,
But suddenly being re-lit five seconds after.

It creeps over the trees,
Knocking them down like a bully,
Pushing through a crowd of kids,
Hurting and terrorizing them.

Something is dragged over the sky,
It's all dark.
Like a lid slammed on the world.

Screams and cries are drained out,
By the rumbling, roaring booms,
Of the thing that has caused miles of damage.

Within a blink of an eye it's gone.
Almost as if it has disappeared into thin air.

**Sarah Tibble  (13)**
**The Atherley School, Southampton**

# Thunderstorm

The cracking, clapping audience announces the roaring
rumbling monster,
approaching into the night.
The black clouds wrap up the world into its lair.
The silver streaks shoot out in all directions lighting
up the world.
The howling wind's like spirits chasing the whistling,
whooshing, whirling rain.
A firework display has begun.
*Strike! Bang! Sizzle! Shoot! Pop! Crack!*
Streams of colours here and there.

A roar, a groan, a rumble, a whistle, a whisper, a drip,
drip, drip . . . silence.
The mysterious powerful creature retreats into its
cave.

**Antonia Dixon  (13)**
**The Atherley School, Southampton**

# Hummingbird

A flutter of wings
Jewel bright
Swift as raindrops
A sight of rapture
To entrap the senses
Of sight and of sound.

The hummingbird flies
Darting among soft flowers
Brushing petals like vibrant silk
The golden sphere of the sun
Warms his racing wings
And lends them their effulgent light.

Sweet ambrosia wafts its scent
Tempting him to a resurgence of effort
To achieve his goal of sustenance.
A delicate pose above the blossom
He takes a drink of sweet delight
And the hummingbird flies, satiated.

**Pippa Janssenswillen (15)**
**Wentworth College, Bournemouth**